JOB

JOB

Peter Bloomfield

EVANGELICAL PRESS
Faverdale North Industrial Estate, Darlington, DL3 0PH, England

Evangelical Press USA
P. O. Box 825, Webster, New York 14580, USA

e-mail: sales@evangelicalpress.org
web: www.evangelicalpress.org

First published 2003

British Library Cataloguing in Publication Data available

ISBN 0 85234 539 9

Printed and bound in Great Britain by Creative Print and Design Wales, Ebbw Vale, South Wales.

CONTENTS

HOW TO USE *THE GUIDE*

Job is the seventh book in a new series called *The Guide*. This series will cover books of the Bible on an individual basis, such as *Colossians and Philemon*, and relevant topics such as *Christian comfort*. The series aim is to communicate the Christian faith in a straightforward and readable way.

Each book in *The Guide* will cover a book of the Bible or topic in some detail, but will be contained in relatively short and concise chapters. There will be questions at the end of each chapter for personal study or group discussion, to help you to study the Word of God more deeply.

An innovative and exciting feature of *The Guide* is that it is linked to its own web site. As well as being encouraged to search God's Word for yourself, you are invited to ask questions related to the book on the web site, where you will not only be able to have your own questions answered, but also be able to see a selection of answers that have been given to other readers. The web site can be found at www.evangelicalpress.org/TheGuide. Once you are on the site you just need to click on the 'select' button at the top of the page, according to the book on which you wish to post a question. Your question will then be answered either by Michael Bentley, the web site co-ordinator and author of *Colossians and Philemon*, or others who have been selected because of their experience, their understanding of the Word of God and their dedication to working for the glory of the Lord.

Other books which have already been published include *Ecclesiastes, The Bible book by book*, *Esther* and topical books on *Revolutionary forgiveness* and *Christian comfort*. Many more will follow. It is the publisher's hope that you will be stirred to think more deeply about the Christian faith, and will be helped and encouraged in living out your Christian life, through the study of God's Word, in the difficult and demanding days in which we live.

CHAPTER ONE

FAITH IN THE FURNACE

LOOK IT UP

BIBLE READING

The book of Job: Overview 1

INTRODUCTION

There is a little song, of human origin, that says:

A little talk with Jesus makes it right, all right
A little talk with Jesus makes it right, all right
In trials of every kind, praise God I always find
A little talk with Jesus makes it right, all right!

But there is a large book of divine origin that suggests the opposite! The book of Job indicates that a little prayer does not solve all problems, even though prayer is certainly vital. This book is a powerful antidote for those well-meant but simplistic answers to the complex problems of life.

Job was suffering terribly. Everything that could go wrong seemed to go wrong. Along came three of his friends who meant well. They wanted to help him sort out his life, but their approach was way off the mark, despite being mixed with some truth, and God rebuked them for it. Their approach was trite and simplistic. It was the 'little talk with Jesus' approach. In essence they said to Job, 'Suffering comes from sin. It's a matter of cause and effect. You are suffering so you must have sinned. So talk to God, own up to your sin, repent of it, and it will be all right.'

But many situations, including Job's, are complex, not simple. Life throws up some questions for which there are no answers. God himself says that Job is a righteous and godly man; yet God allows him to suffer terribly. In fact, God initiated the whole matter by testifying to Job's virtues. 'The LORD said to Satan, "Have you considered my servant Job? There is no one on earth like him; he is blameless and upright, a man who fears God and shuns evil"' (1:8).

God knew this would result in Job's afflictions; so why did he do it? We do not know. No answer is provided in the book, and Job himself never finds out. Life is complex for God's people too! There is no simple explanation for a whole range of human events. There is no way we can find out why many traumas and tragedies occur. There is mystery in providence. There are gaps in our knowledge — massive gaps — and simplistic responses (like those of Job's counsellors) will do more harm than good. They certainly made Job's sufferings even worse, and God rebuked them for it. The church still has an abundant supply of people who trivialize complex problems and give reductionist solutions. The glib solutions just roll off their tongues: 'Claim the promises', 'Let go and let God', 'A little talk with Jesus', 'Jesus is the answer', or 'Just pray about it'!

The book of Job is also a real setback for a modern error known as the 'Prosperity Gospel'. It is promoted by people such as Kenneth and Gloria Copeland, Kenneth Hagin, Brian J. Baker, and Jim and Tammy Bakker. They claim that suffering (pain, failure, hardship and calamity) is not God's will for his people. Typically, Isaiah 53:5, 'By his wounds we are healed,' is misused. Suffering Christians are advised to claim for themselves 'the healing in the atonement'. Various 'healers' say they can banish diseases and injuries (even heart attacks) by simply claiming the power of the blood of Christ.

Gloria Copeland claims: 'You have a title deed to prosperity. Jesus bought and paid for your healing and your salvation. He bore the curse of sin, of sickness and of poverty. When he paid the price for sin, he also paid the price for the curse of poverty so that you can go free.'[1] Kenneth Hagin says that God guarantees four things: protection of yourself and all your property, promotion in your job, prosperity in material things (wealth and success) and perpetuity in all that success.

THINK ABOUT IT

Imagine telling that to Job! He was the godliest man on all the earth, but he lost everything — family, property and livestock

> — and he was covered in loathsome boils from head to toe. To tell Job, 'You shouldn't be suffering, it's not God's will for you', is madness because the first chapter makes it obvious that it *is* God's will. It is God's purpose. God does have a good, wise and rational plan in everything. But he does not always inform us. Why should he?

If you told Job, 'You have a title deed to "prosperity"', he would laugh in your face! If you said to Job, 'If you had enough faith you could be healed, you could prosper, you are guaranteed protection, promotion, prosperity and perpetual success', you would be repeating the same foolish advice given long ago by the prosperity preachers of Job's day: Eliphaz, Bildad and Zophar.

So the book of Job is as modern as today. We need to understand its message if we would be wise. It is part of the 'Wisdom Literature' of the Old Testament, but except for a few well-known verses here and there, it remains a mystery for many. In order to understand it, it is useful to stand back and take in two broad overviews. First, we will deal with what the book teaches, what it puts on the 'agenda'. In the second overview, we will consider how the book unfolds.

Let us first consider what the book of Job teaches, the issues it deals with, namely:

1. The immediate issue (the problem on the surface)
2. The greater issue (the issue below the surface)
3. The ultimate issue (the issue seen in terms of Christ)

WHAT THE TEXT TEACHES

1. The immediate issue

You do not need to be a genius to know that the immediate issue in Job is 'suffering'. But it needs to be more precisely stated. The real issue is *innocent suffering* — the suffering of a godly one — intense suffering that is not due to extensive sin in the sufferer! Why does God allow one of his own people to suffer so horribly? Job was one of God's beloved people. 'In the land of Uz there lived a man whose name was Job. This man was blameless and upright; he feared God and shunned evil' (Job 1:1). So why did he suffer? As we have noted, the question becomes more difficult because God did not merely allow Job to suffer: he actually brought on the suffering (1:8).

God staked his claim on Job's integrity and allowed Satan to hurt him terribly, to prove that his faith is genuine and not out of self-interest. Satan's sinister allegation was that Job only loved God because of what was in it for Job (1:10-12). But the long ordeal proved Job's love was genuine. Job loves God even when it hurts. It is at precisely this point that all of our 'Why?' questions arise.

- Why did God allow that? Indeed, why did God *initiate* the matter?
- Why did God have to prove a point to Satan? (Who cares what Satan thinks?)

- Why hurt a good man in order to win an argument with the evil one?
- Why do it at all? And if there is a good reason, why not let Job know about it ahead of time, so it will comfort and assist him during the trial?

The book of Job never answers these 'Why?' questions. All we know is that Job is not suffering for any wrong he has done. In the prologue we are told what the answer is *not*, but we are never told what it *is*.

An important theological truth ...

God did not merely 'permit' evil, he decreed (purposed) it, making it certain. To God's infinite mind all things are certain before anything exists because he purposes 'whatever comes to pass'. But he is not the author of sin. It is the creature that sins, and not under compulsion, but according to the natural liberty of its will. Every man, angel and demon is a free, responsible and accountable agent. The entire blame for evil belongs to the creature. The entire glory and credit for 'good' belongs to God. Although God decrees both good and evil, his connection to both is not identical. His decree makes both definite. His creation of free agents makes them accountable for their choices. Predestination is not fatalism.

> The notion of God's mere 'permission' fails to explain the origin of evil. If God was free to 'permit' sin, he was also free to 'not permit' sin. But he did not. Why not? The other problem is that it leaves God facing events that he did not purpose. It leaves God facing mere contingencies. It means that there are, after all, mere 'chance' (possible, permissible) events in the universe.

Our problem is that we often become just like Job's counsellors in these kinds of situations. We insist on answers and we find answers. They may even be plausible. But the book of Job alerts us to the fact that sometimes there are no answers, at least not for men. There are gaps in human knowledge, and trying to fill in all the gaps by providing all the answers is disastrous. It removes the need for faith. True godliness means 'We live by faith, not by sight' (2 Corinthians 5:7). Yes, true faith is built upon known facts, real evidences and objective answers to key issues. But once it is established on its concrete foundation, faith is satisfied with that, and it continues to believe even in the void, even in the dark, even when there is confusion, perplexity and hardship such as Job experienced.

What Job's friends did was to take the true principle of cause and effect too far. They took it to its absolute limits. Yes, the Bible *does* acknowledge the truth about cause and effect. 'A man reaps what he sows' (Galatians 6:7). Our sins will find us out (Numbers 32:23). It is true that the way of peace and happiness is to obey God while the way of curse and distress is to disobey. The Old Testament gives many lengthy examples of cause and effect in Israel. The disobedience of God's people repeatedly caused harm. They were overrun by enemies, their crops failed, or there were droughts, blights, mildew and locusts (Deuteronomy 28). When they turned back to the 'ways' of God they had success, blessing, victory and good crops. So the reality of 'cause and effect' is indeed a valid observation.

But it does not always apply. It is not a principle that should be taken to extremes. It does not apply to Job. It does not apply to Abel, or to Uriah the Hittite or to Naboth. Were they murdered because they deserved it? *No.* It does not apply to the man born blind (John 9:1). His lack of sight was not due to his own sin or to any sin by his parents, but to show the power of God.

By taking the true principle of 'cause and effect' to its limits Job's friends alleged that his suffering must have been caused by something he did, some disobedience. So they advised him to own up and get right with God, and that would end it. But God is angry at their answer. He rejects their reasoning.

TO SUMMARIZE

We need to learn from Job, especially in this 'scientific age' of cause and effect. Many of life's problems have no neat 'cause and effect' answers. No amount of scientific effort will change that. God may actually want us to sometimes walk in the shadows, where there is no light, and where there are no answers to the 'Why?' questions. His purpose may be for us to fail, to fall, and to admit, 'I have no idea, I'm lost here.' He may want us to feel our frailty as he nurtures, trains and corrects us. There is a greater issue involved than knowing the answers.

2. The greater issue

What really matters is not knowing the answers but knowing the one who knows all the answers. That is what emerges as the greater issue in this book. The climax of the book comes in Job's final speech in chapter 42. He is still terribly sick, still in a horribly distressed state, when he begins to admit that he has been acting foolishly: 'Surely I spoke of things I did not understand, things too wonderful for me to know' (Job 42:3).

This awareness arose from two magnificent speeches by God from out of the whirlwind (Job 38 and 40:6 - 41:34), where God reminds Job of the inscrutable wonders of his universe. Job is lifted up to see a fresh vision of the profound marvels and the intimidating power of God. He is overwhelmed. All questions now seem puerile.

He shrinks away: 'My ears had heard of you but now my eyes have seen you. Therefore I despise myself and repent in dust and ashes' (42:5-6).

Then God healed Job, restoring his family and fortune. The point is that Job shows us that the great issue in life is to be in communion with God, to know God. Job had been given no more answers to the problems of life. He had no more philosophical clarity about 'suffering' now than he did at the start. What he does have is a new insight into the goodness, the greatness, and the infinite power of God. He acquired that from the word of God (namely, God's speeches in the whirlwind). He was now content to be guided only by the spoken word of God and what it revealed. Though not exhaustive, it is quite sufficient. It does not give all answers to all things, but it reveals God in all his glory. God's word is sufficient for man's faith and life: 'For from him and through him and to him are all things' (Romans 11:36).

Job does not live for 'material things'; they are all taken away. Job does not even live for 'the things of God', the visible comforts and assurances. They are gone too. Even God himself seems far away. Rather, Job lives for the God who transcends time and space and who is really never far away. Thus, being reassured that God is with him, Job's soul rests from turmoil. He has the same blessed mentality as Paul: 'I consider everything a loss compared to the surpassing greatness of knowing Christ Jesus my Lord, for whose sake I have lost all things ... I want to know Christ ... and the fellowship of sharing in his sufferings' (Philippians 3:8-10).

The book of Job exposes the danger that we all face, namely, demanding answers from God before we are prepared to trust him. It is woefully common for men to put God in the witness box for cross-examination, demanding an account of every detailed 'why'. The real issue from this book is: 'Do you trust God simply because he is God? Do you see his incredible majesty, greatness and holiness? Isn't that enough for you?' It is a vital perspective. 'Be still, and know that I am God; I will be exalted among the nations, I will be exalted in the earth' (Psalm 46:10). It is good for us to be well and happy and prosperous. But they are not essential things. The one vital thing is to know God. 'Now this is eternal life: that they may know you, the only true God, and Jesus Christ, whom you have sent' (John 17:3). Job shows us the true priority. If you are well, be well for God's glory. If sick, be sick trusting him. If you die, die to the Lord. Job's faith was in the furnace, but it proved to be pure gold. True faith sometimes staggers under the load, but it staggers in the company of God Almighty who keeps it safe and secure.

3. The ultimate issue

While the book of Job makes good sense when read as a whole and within the Old Testament more broadly, yet its ultimate significance cannot be appreciated without the gospel. All Scripture is pointing to Christ in one way or another. Job is a major Old Testament book where Christ is typified; that is, a shadowy picture is drawn which is more perfectly seen in Christ. How?

Just ask yourself who, ultimately, is the most righteous man on all the earth. Who is the ultimate servant of God? Upon whom does God stake his claim? On whose reputation does the Lord's government of the world rest? The answer in every case is Jesus Christ, the God-man.

Who is it that ultimately suffers terribly but not for any guilt on his part? Who is it that ultimately feels what Job felt — that God was far away, even abandoning him? Who is it that asks the ultimate 'Why?' question: 'My God, my God, *why* have you forsaken me?' It is Jesus, who suffered to vindicate the holy law of God and to save those who deserve to suffer.

In Jesus Christ we see the ultimate and perfect Job. The Christ experience is the Job experience maximized. In Christ we see not only a suffering man, but also the suffering God, the crucified God-man! God himself is the sufferer at Calvary. Never again should Job's complaint be made. There can be no suggestion that God is remote and unconcerned about human suffering. Though it might seem that way to human eyes, the contrary is true. It is clear that God is directly involved. He planned it; he rules and overrules in it; he brings good results from it; and defeats Satan through it.

The cross of Jesus is the ultimate outworking of the message of Job. God planned it. God himself became flesh and blood, entering into the worst miseries of suffering. He brings great fruits out of it and destroys the plans of the evil one. It was Job who said, 'Though he slay me, yet will I hope in him' (Job 13:15). But it was Jesus who proved it to the limit. Jesus demonstrated perfectly that God is to be trusted, come what may! One thing mattered to Jesus: 'Yet not what I will, but what you will' (Mark 14:36).

The book closes with God telling Job's friends to go and honour Job, to confess their sins, and that Job will act as their mediator and priest, leading to their forgiveness. 'My servant Job will pray for you, and I will accept his prayer and not deal with you according to your folly' (42:8). This is typical of Christ, our great priest and mediator. He lives to pray for us, and God grants his prayers. The ultimate issue is not so much 'What do you think about Job?', but 'What do you think about Christ?', for Job foreshadows Christ. It is a very profitable and practical book, helping us to cope with very significant issues in life.

QUESTIONS FOR DISCUSSION

1. *Read Hebrews 11:1-6. What is the connection between faith and understanding? Does it agree*

with Anselm's dictum, Credo, ut intelligam *(I believe in order that I might understand)?*

2. *Read Luke 24:25-27 and 44-46. In that light, is it true to say, 'Without knowing Christ you cannot understand the Old Testament'?*

3. *Use Romans 8:35-39 and Hebrews 12:1-12 to answer the following: Is suffering to be expected for Christians? Does it mean our faith is too weak? Is it God's will that we should always prosper?*

4. *Read Proverbs 16:4; Daniel 4:34-35; and Ephesians 1:11. Do they describe God's sovereign rule as 'permission' or 'predestination'?*

THE GUIDE

CHAPTER TWO

JOB: THE LITERARY MASTERPIECE

LOOK IT UP

BIBLE READING

The book of Job: Overview 2

INTRODUCTION

Thomas Carlyle spoke for many people when he said about the book of Job, 'There is nothing written, I think, in the Bible or out of it, of equal literary merit.'[1] It is a masterly combination of mostly poetry, with prose at the beginning and end, that makes the struggles of Job so vivid and real to the reader. It is a masterpiece at creating 'reader involvement'. Our deepest emotions are affected. It prompts us ask the most fundamental questions. Job is a man who gains our admiration one moment, and our astonishment the next. He is so great, yet he is so ordinary. He shows the sort of faith we all aspire to, but he also shows the sorts of weaknesses we are all familiar with. It is also a masterpiece in the way it reveals almighty God. He is immense in power, always in control, yet gentle with his people. Few books present the intimidating greatness of God so brilliantly as Job, especially the dramatic 'whirlwind' speeches.

All good works of art need to be seen in their proper light. As a good painting is set off and appreciated by a quality frame around it, so is a good book. We will not appreciate this literary gem without the correct framework. We need to see it as a whole. We need to know as much as possible about when, where, and why it was written, about how it opens up, its arrangement and structure, and some of its subtle features. Three questions will help us to stand back and appreciate the book of Job as a literary unit.

1. What setting?
2. What structure?
3. What sympathies?

1. What setting?

The opening verse tells us that Job lived in the land of Uz (where the action of the book took place). We cannot 'pinpoint' where this was with certainty, but the most likely place is the area just below the Dead Sea, in between Edom and North Arabia. There are several things that indicate this. Firstly, Job's three friends came to him from this general area. For example, Eliphaz came from Teman, a well-known locality in Edom. Secondly, it is consistent with the attacks described in chapter 1: raiders came from the Sabeans (Bedouins from Arabia) and Assyrians (Chaldeans) from Mesopotamia. Then the book of Lamentations (4:21) associates Uz with Edom. 'Rejoice and be glad, O Daughter of Edom, you who live in the land of Uz,' implying strongly that it was called Uz before the Edomites came in. And in

Jeremiah 25:20-21 it is mentioned in connection with a broad sweep of nations, Philistia, Edom, Ammon and Moab, indicating an area stretching SW-SE of the Dead Sea. It does not seem that Job was a Jew. He was 'from the East', that is, he was across the Jordan, not in the land of Israel.

The man

Job was a true historical person. Ezekiel 14:14 lists three great men of God together, 'Noah, Daniel and Job'. Clearly, Job is just as much a historical fact as Noah and Daniel. The New Testament also regards him as historically real as the prophets. 'As an example of patience in the face of suffering, take the prophets who spoke in the name of the Lord... You have heard of Job's perseverance and have seen what the Lord finally brought about' (James 5:10-11).

There's a lot at stake here!

The historical reliability of the Bible is an essential (and well-attested) part of Christian faith. But there are warnings to heed in defending it. First, we must never forget that scepticism is ultimately a spiritual problem:

'The man without the Spirit does not accept the things that come from the Spirit of God' (1 Corinthians 2:14). We must not hesitate in presenting men with all the compelling evidence for confidence in the Bible, but we dare not assume man's autonomous ability to accept it. Until he is born again, he remains blind to the facts. But keep telling him the facts anyway. They are the only things entitled to a hearing!

Then there is the danger of zeal without knowledge. The reliability of a text is not a matter of crass literalism! The various literary forms (like poetry, proverb, prose and parable) must be taken as intended. Psalm 97:5 is perfectly reliable though not historically literal when it tells us 'the mountains melt like wax'. Christians do more harm than good if they assume the Bible is to be taken as 'literal where possible'. Rather, it is to be taken as literal where the genre is literal, poetic where it is poetry, and figurative or illustrative or anthropomorphic where the context requires it. Yes, Jesus was surrounded by 'many strong bulls of Bashan' (Psalm 22:12). That is the historic truth of Calvary, but the bulls were literally men!

The times

When did Job live and the events described in this book happen? And when was the book written, and by whom? It is hard to be dogmatic about when Job lived.

There are various credible opinions. However, we are restricted to the internal evidence of the book, which, on balance, points to a patriarchal setting. So the events took place in the pre-Mosaic, pre-Israelite, pre-Sinai period of covenant history, somewhere in the age of Abraham, Isaac and Jacob, up to Joseph. Broadly that is between 1950 B.C. and 1600 B.C. What is the evidence?

- Job is introduced as a 'patriarchal' type in chapter 1, operating as the head of his family or clan in a way far more reminiscent of Abraham's time than later.

- He acts as 'priest' for the family, interceding for them with sacrificial burnt offerings for their sins (1:5), just as other patriarchs like Noah and Abraham did (Genesis 8:20; 22:13). Job's three counsellors also offered sacrifices by their own hand (Job 42). After the events on Mount Sinai, the Mosaic Law created a distinct class of priests to do this. Job fits best into the pre-Mosaic culture.

- The longevity of Job is consistent with the patriarchal period. He lived another 140 years after the Lord restored him (42:16) and since he had ten grown-up children, each living in their own 'family' house, it is reasonable to assume he was between fifty and sixty years old at the start. So he died at about 190-200 years of age. By comparison, Abraham lived 175 years.

- The divine name 'Shaddai' שַׁדַּי (Almighty), so characteristic of the patriarchs, occurs thirty-one times in Job and only sixteen times in the rest of the Old Testament. There are no references to Israel, the Exodus, or Moses or the Mosaic Law, or to the tabernacle. This is not conclusive in itself but it is most consistent with the patriarchal period.

Regarding authorship, there is a tremendous variety of opinion. Some say the writer is Job himself (about 1900 B.C.), some say it was Moses (about 1400 B.C.), some say Solomon (about 900 B.C.), or Isaiah (about 700 B.C.), or Jeremiah or Baruch (about 600 B.C.), while others say it was Ezra the scribe (about 500-400 B.C.). In favour of Moses is the fact that the land of Uz is adjacent to Midian (where Moses lived forty years prior to leading Israel in the Exodus). It is therefore conceivable that Moses obtained a record of the story left in manuscripts by Job or Elihu, putting it into the format of the present book.

My own conclusion is that the writer was Job himself, the same man who lived about 4000 years ago in the time of Abraham. It seems that he wrote the original book (perhaps with Elihu's help), having 140 years to do so. Of course someone younger (again, perhaps Elihu) added the last lines recording Job's death. The great detail of the debates between Job and his friends would virtually demand that the writer was actually involved in the experiences now recorded. Consistent with this is Job's heartfelt cry in the midst of his terrible ordeal: 'Oh, that my words were recorded, that they were written on a scroll, that they were inscribed with an iron tool on lead, or engraved in rock for ever!' (19:23-24).

Job probably did not expect to survive the ordeal, so he did not expect to see his desire for a permanent record come to fruition. But, after God restored and vindicated him before his friends and enemies and Satan, it would have been natural for Job to write the book while it was still vivid in his memory. Indeed, one can hardly imagine him not fulfilling that strong desire during the 140 years of his new life! It is possible that Job did not write it in Hebrew, but that Moses or another, centuries later, saw the magnificent value of it and copied it into Hebrew from Job's original (which is now lost). So Job is probably the oldest book in the Bible, about 500 years older than the books of Moses.

THINK ABOUT IT

An interesting implication.

The early human race was far from 'primitive'. In his famous poem on wisdom (chapter 28)

Job describes underground mining for precious ores and stones. Men already understood many geological distinctions: Job mentions gold, iron, copper, silver, onyx, sapphire, coral, jasper, topaz and rubies. Man was already familiar with technologies like smelting the ore, cutting shafts deep underground, illuminating the darkest recesses of earth, and damming up rivers. Adam's immediate descendants had skills including animal husbandry, music and metal manufacturing (Genesis 4:20-22). We need to constantly resist the prejudices of secular education based on an evolutionary approach to history and anthropology.

2. What structure?

The book is structured into three sections.

1. *The prologue,* consisting of the first two chapters. The style is *prose* (ordinary historical narrative). Here the scene is set, and earthly and heavenly realities are placed side by side.

2. *The epilogue* (42:7-14). This is also *prose.* It closes the book, bringing the whole story to a glorious conclusion.

3. *The dialogue* (3:1 - 42:6). This is mostly *poetry* and takes up the great majority of the book. It records the

exchanges and counter exchanges between Job and his three friends. It also records the four speeches of Elihu, which are not responded to by either Job or God. It includes the climactic whirlwind speeches of God, leading Job to a renewed contentment, humility and zeal for God. A brief summary of each section is useful.

The prologue section

This is essential to the impact of the book, because it informs the reader that the imminent sufferings of Job are *not* due to any fault in him. Only the reader is privy to this fact: neither Job nor his friends knew this information during the long ordeal. So the prologue gives us a preview from the heavenly perspective of what happens to Job on earth. Job's sufferings here on earth result from a disagreement in the heavenly realms between God and Satan. The issue at stake is whether a man is capable of loving God sincerely. Does Job love God simply because he is God, or is it because of the benefits received?

Satan's charge (1:9-11) alleges that there is no such thing as genuine, unselfish love for God among men: even in the best of men, godliness is motivated by self-interest — an attitude of 'What's in it for me?' And the acid test is Job, the most righteous man in his day. So God set up the test to prove Satan wrong (1:12). In effect

God told Satan, 'Take away the blessings I gave Job, and see how he still loves me.'

Though Satan is ruthless, swift and thorough, he is annoyed that Job remains loyal to God. God mocks Satan and boasts in the integrity of Job (2:3). Satan is permitted to test Job more severely (v. 6) and smites him with an intolerable and loathsome disease — painful sores from the soles of his feet to the crown of his head; but still in vain. Three friends, Eliphaz, Bildad and Zophar, heard of the tragedy and visited Job. They were horrified at the spectacle: 'They could hardly recognize him; they began to weep aloud, and they tore their robes and sprinkled dust on their heads' (v. 12). They were *silent* for seven days and nights. 'No one said a word to him, because they saw how great his suffering was' (2:13).

The dialogue section

Job breaks the silence with a soliloquy (chapter 3). It is a lament, a cry of pain, cursing the day he was born. Then there are three cycles of speeches. In the first two cycles (chapters 4-21) the friends speak in turn and a reply from Job follows each one. In the third cycle (chapters 22-27) only two friends speak and Job replies to each of them. The friends always speak in the same order (probably reflecting their ages): Eliphaz, then Bildad, then Zophar, and their speeches all rest on the assumption that Job has brought the sufferings on himself.

Each cycle becomes more critical of Job. Initially more polite and guarded, the criticisms develop into open confrontation. Eliphaz is the gentlest of the three, while Zophar is the sharpest, coarsest and most dogmatic. As readers, we are inevitably 'involved'. On the one hand, we know from the prologue that Job is right and the three friends are wrong. We get quite annoyed as they misuse a true principle in a situation where it does not apply. Job endures their repeated thesis that *phenomenal suffering is due to phenomenal sin in the sufferer*. And he denies it repeatedly. With the advantage of hindsight, modern readers can wonder what these three would have said to Jesus on the cross. His was phenomenal suffering in phenomenal innocence. So we will try to defend Job.

On the other hand, our 'hero' sometimes embarrasses us. He says some very foolish and ill-advised things, although he later regrets doing so. The three 'friends' are quite right when they rebuke Job about those things. The reader cannot help agreeing with them. The situation gets terribly tense. We cannot read with apathy. We feel the heat of battle. That is why chapter 28 is so welcome, an artistic interlude built in by the skilful author. A magnificent poem on the elusiveness of wisdom and its true sources, the tranquility of this meditation contrasts with the turbulence before and after it, providing welcome relief for the reader.

Then we come to the two most stupendous moments in the book. We see Job's final 'intrepid challenge' where he begs God to answer him (chapters 29 - 31), and God's dramatic, powerful and awesome replies (chapters 38 - 41). In between them comes another tranquil break, another rest from the turmoil. We hear a new and fascinating character, Elihu, making four speeches (chapters 32 - 37). He freshens the air with a far more perceptive and accurate view than the others. He essentially tells Job that he needs to humble himself before God and submit to God's process of purifying his life through trials and hardships. Job came to agree with that.

Significantly, God does not rebuke Elihu as he did the others. As we shall discover, Elihu's speeches are quite profound. They accord with the mind of God and they answer Job's needs. They provide the ideal prelude for the momentous whirlwind speeches of God that follow.

The epilogue section

Job agrees he has spoken out of line. He marvels at how great God is and how small *he* is. And though he is still terribly ill and in great pain, that seems more remote, for now he is in the shadow of the Almighty. The intimidating greatness of God makes other things (including sickness) of little consequence. Then God heals him and blesses him, and honours and vindicates him. Satan is defeated, conspicuous by his absence from the scene. It is the day of glory for God and his faithful ones.

3. What sympathies?

The reader is unavoidably drawn in. The book is so brilliantly written that we must take sides. It is natural to feel sympathy towards Job and anger for his three counsellors. Lest we overdo it, some salutary observations are appropriate.

1. Avoid over-glamorizing Job!

Do not make him larger than life. Do not exaggerate his virtues! He is truly a great man of faith, but his initial righteousness moves more and more into self-righteousness. Elihu quite correctly rebukes Job for this: 'But you have said in my hearing — I heard the very words — "I am pure and without sin; I am clean and free from guilt. Yet God has found fault with me; he considers me his enemy"' (33:8-10). Indeed, God rebukes Job for this: 'Would you discredit my justice? Would you condemn me to justify yourself?' (40:8).

But Job owns up. He repents. He changes, and to his credit, he does it in the midst of suffering! It is the furnace of affliction that brings out the dross in Job's gold, leaving him purer than before. There are other faults in Job, as we shall see. To be blind to them means to miss some of the major comforts of the book, driving Job far away from 'us' and our struggles. It makes him 'superhuman', and irrelevant to us, when in fact, he is very human, and frail, and prone to err. But he is kept by God's power so that neither Satan, nor sickness, nor foolish speeches can make his salvation fail.

2. On the other hand, do not demonize Job's advisers!

Do not make them worse than the facts demand. For all their faults they are still Job's true friends. Of all who knew Job and his calamity, they at least came to him. They visited him. They sympathized and wanted to relieve and console him. They mourned with him silently for seven days. They were moved and shaken by his burdens. They did not advise Job as foolishly as his wife did: 'Curse God and die!' They had the courage to confront Job face to face rather than whisper behind his back. They are well grounded in theological truths, consistently defending the honour and integrity of God. They defend his sovereign rights. They will not tolerate a slur upon God's name. If there is any sin and curse and anguish in this world, they will not impute it to God!

These are very good attributes! If only more men had this courage! They were not so soppy and sentimental as to overlook the foolish speeches of a sick man. However, whether he was sick or not, when Job casts a shadow over God's reputation, intentional or otherwise, he must be warned.

DISCUSS IT

QUESTIONS FOR DISCUSSION

1. *Read Job 19:23-24. Why do you think it was so important to Job that his ordeal should be recorded?*

2. *Read John chapter 9. What similarities exist between that story and Job's?*

3. *Read Ephesians 4:29; James 1:19; and Proverbs 17:28 and 18:2. How did the speeches of Job's counsellors measure up?*

THE GUIDE

CHAPTER THREE

SATAN PROPERLY ASSESSED

LOOK IT UP

BIBLE READING

Job 1 - 2

INTRODUCTION

The book of Job introduces us to Satan at the very outset. Twice in the prologue we are shown the activities of the invisible, spiritual world. Twice we are shown how the angels come to present themselves before the Lord. So far, so good! But what startles us is the comment that 'Satan also came with them' (1:6; 2:1). He did not sneak in under cover. He did not disguise himself as 'an angel of light'. He is openly and literally described as 'the Satan' (הַשָּׂטָן). Here is 'the adversary' of God and man. Here is a mere servant of God, appearing one day with all the other servants of God, to offer homage to God, to receive his commission, and to give account for his actions.

This picture of Satan seems so incongruous with the Satan we know from the rest of the Bible that some interpreters have maintained that the 'Satan' in Job is not the same as Satan elsewhere! How could that evil being have a place among 'the Sons of God' (בְּנֵי הָאֱלֹהִים)? How could he come at the stated times and present himself and show submission before almighty God? How can this be said of such a despicable and vile enemy of God?

However, a closer look will show us that this harmonizes perfectly with the rest of Scripture. This 'Satan' is not some other being, not some misnamed angel. This is *the* evil one, the fallen archangel, and the reason he appears openly before God is not because he wants to (as the other angels do), but because he has to! He presents himself, acknowledging God's sovereignty on the throne of the cosmos, because despite all Satan's evil desires and intentions to dethrone God, he cannot!

REMEMBER THIS

What a comforting truth!

Satan is a mere servant of God. He ends up doing the will of God (against his own will). Satan is accountable to God and limited and hemmed in by God. Satan is completely outgunned. He is not a law unto himself. He is not competent to do all he maliciously desires. Evil is in the world, but evil is not out of control.

Yes, there is a real personal being known as 'Satan'. A Bible believer cannot deny that or depersonalize evil as a mere 'force'. But even believers can believe wrongly, by believing too much or too little about Satan.

Believers can have an inadequate understanding of what they believe. Job chapters 1 and 2 provide a good starting point for a proper assessment of Satan. In broad theological terms, that means having a balanced view of two things:

1. Satanic potency (his real power)
2. Satanic impotency (his real limits and restraints)

1. Satanic potency

It is dangerous and foolish to underestimate an enemy, especially this one! Indeed the Bible insists we wake up and take a sober view: 'Be self-controlled and alert. Your enemy the devil prowls around like a roaring lion looking for someone to devour' (1 Peter 5:8). We need to be alert to several facts about Satan.

- He has all the powers of an archangel gone wrong. He intends our doom, and he hesitates at nothing to ruin us. There is nothing too evil for him to relish. He pursues mischievous plans with sleepless vigilance. He does not grow weary in doing evil, as we grow weary in doing well. He feeds on evil. His appetite for it is voracious and insatiable.

- He is invisible, and so he has all the advantages of secrecy, taking victims by surprise.

- He leads a vast army of superhuman thugs, the demons, who cast their lot in with him at the Fall. They love him as their prince. They are fanatically united in his evil cause, with all the rage and cunning of Beelzebub.

- Satan has power over the bodies as well as the minds of men. This is implied in the terrible afflictions he put on Job: 'So Satan went out from the presence of the LORD and afflicted Job with painful sores from the soles of his feet to the top of his head' (2:7). In his first vain assault on Job, Satan stirred up vicious marauding gangs of Sabeans and Chaldeans to smite Job's family. He also acted supernaturally, reported by a witness with the words: 'The fire of God fell from the sky and burned up the sheep and the servants' (1:16). This is what Revelation 13:13 refers to when it describes the Satanic Beast who 'performed great and miraculous signs, even causing fire to come down from heaven to earth in full view of men'.

- Satan can possess people, taking up residence, touching their deep inner reality, giving them brute strength and madness of mind, causing them to foam at the mouth and dash themselves against rocks (see Mark 5:1-20).

- Satan's fearful potency is symbolized by the biblical image of the fiery red dragon, with seven heads and ten horns, and seven crowns on his heads, his tail sweeping across the heavens and throwing a third of the stars to earth. His posture is that of crouching viciously to devour the Christ child. Satan is enraged in his vain persecution of the church of God. But he never appears to men as this hideous monster. He prefers to be disguised as an 'angel of light' (2 Corinthians 11:14). His salesmen are also 'wolves in sheep's clothing'. 'For Satan himself masquerades as an angel of light. It is not surprising, then, if his servants masquerade as servants of righteousness' (11:14-15). Today the satanic hosts appear as 'Christians', preachers, ordained pastors, evangelists, gifted academics, scholars, and generous people. As a result, gullible people are hospitable and receptive to their poisonous doctrines.

The favourite ploy of the devil is to pretend he *is* Christ, to appear *as* Christ. That kills more souls than outright opposition to Christ. The term 'Antichrist' in the New Testament literally means 'in the place of Christ'. Paul explicitly warns us of Satan's power and tells us to assess him properly. We dare not underestimate 'the work of Satan displayed in all kinds of counterfeit miracles, signs and wonders, and in every sort of evil that deceives those who are perishing. They perish because they refused to love the truth and so be saved' (2 Thessalonians 2:9-10).

The Bible shows that Satan has terrible power over men!

- He blinds their minds: 'The god of this age has blinded the minds of unbelievers, so that they cannot see the light of the gospel' (2 Corinthians 4:4).

- He snatches the Word of God away: 'This is the meaning of the parable: The seed is the word of God. Those along the path are the ones who hear, and then the devil comes and takes away the word from their hearts, so that they may not believe and be saved' (Luke 8:11-12). What terrible, devilish power! He kicks men when they are already down!

Don't fall for it!

Satan's most effective trick is to convince people that he does not exist. That is why he attacks the Bible. It reveals and unmasks him. The Bible prints his mug-shot! But once men deny his existence they are 'sitting ducks' for the rest of Satan's deceitful schemes. They see him as a mere figment of the imagination. In fact they are imagining a figment!

- He controls men so they become miniature replicas of him. They become implacably hateful to Christ and the gospel, like Elymas the magician. Paul told him: 'You are a child of the devil and an enemy of everything that is right! You are full of all kinds of deceit and trickery. Will you never stop perverting the right ways of the Lord?' (Acts 13:10). Likewise, Jesus described the Pharisees and Scribes as the very offspring of Satan: 'You belong to your father, the devil, and you want to carry out your father's desire' (John 8:44). Christ spoke plainly: woe to such hypocrites! Like Satan, they appear good on the outside but they are rotten on the inside. They are blind guides, fools, serpents, and a real brood of vipers!

Finally, we must not think that as Christians we have nothing more to worry about from Satan, as if he is kept away from us. Are we more acceptable to God than Job was? No, so remember what Satan did to Job and be careful. After all, it is to Christians that Peter writes: 'Your adversary the devil prowls around like a roaring lion seeking someone to devour.' James tells Christians: 'Resist the devil, and he will flee from you' (James 4:7). We need to resist because he will assault us. Jesus tells even the Apostle: 'Satan has asked to sift you as wheat' (Luke 22:31).

When he said, 'I will build my church and the gates of hell will not prevail', Jesus implied that the gates of hell will do everything possible to harm the church. It is to true Christians that Paul insists: 'Put on the full armour of God so that you can take your stand against the devil's schemes. For our struggle is not against flesh and blood, but against the rulers, against the authorities, against the powers of this dark world and against the spiritual forces of evil in the heavenly realms' (Ephesians 6:11-12). The hymn puts it aptly: 'Soldiers of Christ arise and put your armour on!' Satan's fiery darts are not merely aimed at God's elect, they are particularly focused on them. Satan wants us in hell and he works overtime to achieve it. He is potent! Only a fool denies it.

2. Satanic impotency

Paradoxically, it is the terrible power of Satan that makes him so puny! Before God the omnipotent, Satan is impotent. He is powerless whenever, however, and wherever God determines. To demonstrate this, observe the cynical power of Satan's allegations about Job.

Satan denies that anything or anyone is genuinely good: not Job, not even God! So he asks the cynical question: 'Does Job fear God for nothing?' (1:9). During his 'roaming through the earth and going to and fro in it' (1:7) Satan regularly sees plenty of religious sham and hypocrisy. He knows that genuine godliness is rare. He has seen plenty of people *in* religion only for what they can get *out* of it. Moreover, Satan knows that God agrees. He knows God's complaints in Scripture of 'lip service', and of 'vain', 'empty' external worship. He speaks of 'hearts far from him'. Doesn't the parable of the sower teach that some receive the word, and they grow for a while, but cares, worries and trials wither them up? They really have no heart for God's word. They are a sham.

So, Satan knows how hurtful his cynical remark is. In effect he says that Job's godliness is artificial, having never been tested by a trial. And he implies God is no better! God allegedly makes it easy for Job because that makes it easy for God too. Satan claims God has secured Job's loyalty by 'bribery', giving him plenty of gifts and sheltering him from harm. Satan suggests a test to prove the point: 'Stop being good to Job! Stop wrapping him in cotton wool! Cause a calamity to befall him, then watch him cave in.'

Notice God's reaction! He is neither perplexed nor threatened. He does not call all the holy angels for a 'think tank', a summit meeting to plan what to do next. He does not tell them to go and surround Job and look after him. Indeed, he does not even see the need to forewarn Job in any way. He does not tell Job that he is going to suffer for a while, but 'Hang in there, I'll keep you!' No, God is the omnipotent sovereign king. In the face of all the ranting and raving of powers in heaven and hell, God is undisturbed: 'The One enthroned in heaven laughs; the Lord scoffs at them' (Psalm 2:4).

At first God says to Satan, 'Very well, then, everything he has is in your hands, but on the man himself do not lay a finger' (1:12). When Satan failed to undo Job's faith God raised the matter again. He gave Satan absolute freedom to do anything he liked with Job (apart from killing him). Again Satan was thoroughly frustrated in his failure. Potency is impotency in the face of omnipotence. Even when Satan is allowed to give full vent to his malicious power against God and his saints, he cannot do anything to hinder their faith or God's kingdom. God causes all things, even evil things, to work together for the good of those who love him (Romans 8:28). God will derive glory and honour even from Satan.

Surely we love the omnipotence of God! How it thrills our souls! Look at the wise way he defeats Satan, not simply by rushing upon him, not by knocking him out or obliterating him with an omnipotent avalanche of infinite horsepower! No! Far more gloriously, God does it by putting weapons into Satan's hands, by granting him time and place and freedom to engage all his cunning and malice, and having done it all, to destroy him with the breath of his mouth. 'And then the lawless one will be revealed, whom the Lord Jesus will overthrow with the breath of his mouth and destroy by the splendour of his coming' (2 Thessalonians 2:8).

Martin Luther said it well:

And though this world with devils filled
Should threaten to undo us

We will not fear for God has willed
His truth to triumph through us
The Prince of darkness grim,
We tremble not for him;
His rage we can endure,
For lo! His doom is sure,
One little word will fell him.[1]

Meanwhile Satan is caused to facilitate the very good that he hates! In shaking Job, he establishes him more firmly. In trying to move Job away from God, he only anchors him more securely. In persecuting the martyrs he only inspires many more to believe. In killing the Head of the Church he only ensures the eternal life of the whole body. Biting the heel of that one seed of the woman only ensures the salvation of a great multitude no man can number. By raging against the spark of faith in twelve disciples he fanned the gospel into a bush fire, blazing into every continent in every age thereafter.

Satan introduces heretics into the church: an Arian here, a Jesuit there, a Socinian, a Unitarian, a Modalist, and a great many others besides, intending to confuse the truth with error. And he only succeeds in forcing the champions and intellectual giants of God's church to rise up and write great creeds and statements that declare the truth of God more precisely and beautifully: an Augustine, a Calvin, a Westminster Assembly, or a Synod of Dort. The more frantically the gates of hell rage against Christ, the more impotent the gates of hell are seen to be!

What conclusions are in order? What is the right Christian response to Satan? Firstly, do not ever underestimate the power and evil scheming of Satan. It is by a proper biblical assessment and knowledge of Satan that we will give him no opportunity, 'in order that Satan might not outwit us. For we are not unaware of his schemes' (2 Corinthians 2:11). Secondly, have nothing to do with satanic, evil, occult things. Abstain and flee from spiritism, mediums, occult 'games', witchcraft and witches, ouija boards, séances, demonic films, ghosts and ghouls. The right way to learn about Satan is by sound Bible teaching and in no other way. The evil one does not give good teaching about evil. Thirdly, resist Satan strongly: 'Resist the devil, and he will flee from you' (James 4:7). Every sin is his opportunity so, 'Do not give the devil a foothold' (Ephesians 4:27). We resist Satan best by constantly growing more mature as a Christian.

We must not overestimate Satan either. He is totally hemmed in by God. He is a mere fallen creature of God. Satan is a fallen angel not a fallen god! The God who made him out of nothing can just as easily snuff him out! But the Lord of Hosts rules and overrules in all the malicious deeds of Satan to manifest his own glory. Do not see 'demons' behind every tree. Do not give Satan more significance than the Bible does. Do not neglect the sinfulness of men by inventing scapegoat demons, like the 'demons' of gluttony, immorality, drugs, debt or smoking.

Remember, the Christian is a soldier. Just as God left a remnant of Canaanites in the promised land to teach succeeding generations that they must defend their God-given treasures and keep fighting the enemy, so we too must 'contend for the faith that was once for all entrusted to the saints' (Jude 3). It is perplexing that people still do not realize that Satan presents himself with the sons of God now in the church as much as he did in Job's day! Why do people marvel and complain that there are disputes and battles in presbytery and assembly? When voices in the church tell us the Bible is not true, and God is not the Creator, and our schools may teach Darwinian evolution as a credible explanation of origins, and homosexuality is acceptable, it is time to recognize Satan in the midst. It is time for soldiers to get up and fight him and his false prophets. Good men must draw out the sharp two-edged sword and cut off all wickedness from amongst us. We cannot be the church triumphant till Christ returns. Until then we must be the church militant.

QUESTIONS FOR DISCUSSION

1. *From Ephesians 6:10-18, what truths can we learn about men and Satan?*

2. *Read Revelation 20:1-10. How does it help us to assess Satan?*

CHAPTER FOUR

JOB PROPERLY ASSESSED

LOOK IT UP

BIBLE READING

Job 29 - 30

INTRODUCTION

The various historical persons and events of the Old Testament are not recorded merely to inform us of the past; they equip us for the present and future. They are 'useful for teaching, rebuking, correcting and training in righteousness, so that the man of God may be thoroughly equipped for every good work' (2 Timothy 3:16-17). Whether it is about Noah or Adam or Jonah or Job or Satan, we must understand: 'These things happened to them as examples and were written down as warnings for us, on whom the fulfilment of the ages has come' (1 Corinthians 10:11). The New Testament specifically names Job as someone to emulate.

When James wrote to God's oppressed and persecuted people, they were being cheated by their employers. Their wages were not being paid and they were unable to get justice from the courts. James advised them: 'Brothers, as an example of patience in the face of suffering, take the prophets who spoke in the name of the Lord.

As you know, we consider blessed those who have persevered. You have heard of Job's perseverance and have seen what the Lord finally brought about. The Lord is full of compassion and mercy' (James 5:10-11). It is assumed that we will make a proper assessment of men such as Job, learning from their good example how to endure under trial. Following the advice of the New Testament, we can properly assess Job by considering two main issues:

1. Job's great sufferings
2. Job's godly response

1. Job's great sufferings

Job's sufferings arose from Satan's cynical claim that there is no such thing as sincere godliness. Even in Job (the best man on earth according to God), faithfulness is only a refined form of selfishness. Job is only looking after himself! That is the charge. So Satan dared God to remove Job's comforts to prove the point. Job was severely afflicted. The severity lies in the combination of three things.

First, Job was unaware of this dispute in the spiritual realm between God and Satan. He was unaware of both Satan's malicious designs and God's complete confidence in Job. The sufferings of Job happened suddenly, out of the blue, unannounced and unexpected. It is only we readers of the book who are privy to the whole picture. His ordeal would have been severe even if Job had known these things. But at least that information would have helped him to grit his teeth, batten down the hatches, and hold fast to God, knowing the trust that God had placed in him. So his sufferings were aggravated by his innocent ignorance.

A second factor was the inequality of the contest. Job was a great man, but only a man. Satan is much more powerful, having all the resources of a fallen archangel. Invisible and untiring, he can perform signs and wonders and possess human minds. He is a much stronger warrior than Job. The Bible calls him the 'ruler of the kingdom of the air'; 'an enormous red dragon with seven heads and ten horns and seven crowns on his heads. His tail swept a third of the stars out of the sky and flung them to the earth'; that enraged ravenous beast 'who prowls around like a roaring lion looking for someone to devour' (Ephesians 2:2; Revelation 12:3-4; 1 Peter 5:8).

Thirdly, Job was a pioneer. He went where no one had gone before. He had none of the many supports and consolations now available to suffering saints. He had no book of Job to draw help from. He had no Bible books at all! (Remember, Job is possibly the oldest book in the Old Testament.) Job had never heard about Calvary, and Gethsemane, and a Saviour touched with the feeling of our infirmities. There was no

Romans chapter 8 reassuring him that 'God works for the good of those who love him' (v. 28). There was no comforting word from a fellow sufferer like Paul, saying, 'I consider that our present sufferings are not worth comparing with the glory that will be revealed in us' (8:18). There was no Peter assuring him that it is blessed to 'suffer for doing good and you endure it, this is commendable before God. To this you were called, because Christ suffered for you, leaving you an example, that you should follow in his steps' (1 Peter 2:20-21). Job had none of that. He had no 'Sermon on the Mount', no Beatitudes to assure him 'Blessed are you when people insult you, persecute you and falsely say all kinds of evil against you because of me ... great is your reward in heaven' (Matthew 5:11-12).

Imagine the loneliness!

Job did not have a great cloud of witnesses who had gone before him (he had no Hebrews 11). Job was a pioneer, a trailblazer. He suffered alone. He had no role models to look up to. He had no chart to guide him. He was passing through an oppressive, violent, tangled and uncleared jungle! What a man! Every weary traveller since then has been greatly helped by Job. So, a new lesson was being given to the world, and Job was the medium of instruction.

As we now retrace those terrible steps, we can see three stages, each one increasingly painful and severe.

Stage 1: In one awful day he was deprived of all his possessions. He awoke that morning to cloudless blue skies, but suddenly it changed to darkness and gloom. He arose that morning with every reason to feel secure. He enjoyed a prosperous abundance from God. He was highly esteemed by everyone. No one begrudged Job his wealth, apart from Satan. Job's 'good old days' are described vividly as he wistfully recalls life before the bomb fell: 'How I long for … the days when God watched over me … when my path was drenched with cream and the rock poured out for me streams of olive oil … the young men saw me and stepped aside and the old men rose to their feet; the chief men refrained from speaking and covered their mouths with their hands … Whoever heard me spoke well of me … because I rescued the poor who cried for help … I made the widow's heart sing. I put on righteousness as my clothing … I was eyes to the blind and feet to the lame. I was a father to the needy' (29:2-16). Job quite expected to end his days in this same way, happy, loved and respected. 'I thought, "I shall die in my own house, my days as numerous as the grains of sand … My glory will remain fresh in me, the bow ever new in my hand"' (29:18-20).

But within twelve hours, everything was gone! Can you possibly imagine that trauma? Like a naked babe, Job was helpless, destitute and powerless; at the mercy of surroundings. Each piece of bad news was followed by something worse! It might have been more bearable if the calamity was not so sweeping and so universal, if something was spared, just a part of his property for consolation. But nothing was left. And then his dearest possessions, his children, were all gone in a single day! Not one, or two, or three, or seven, or nine, but all ten of them! Worse, all the grandchildren were killed too, and all at once! Had even one remained to comfort Job it would be something — but none! If only the blows had not fallen in such quick succession, if there was a lull of mercy, even a little time to prepare for the next shock, some interlude of relief to summon new strength — but no! Job's experience was an avalanche of horror.

Stage 2: A blow upon his person now aggravates the heavy blow on his possessions. As if he was not in enough misery already, intense physical illness and pain came over him. The outward symptoms are extremely gruesome; we can only imagine the inward effects of his torment. There were painful sores all over his body, but there were no doctors in those days; no medication, no chemist, no drugs, and no hospitals. The 'treatment' (hardly therapeutic) was a piece of broken pottery for Job to scrape himself as he sat in the ashes. It was a wretched scene, a man beside himself with gnawing pain. No doubt he opened up many sores and made them worse. Infections would follow. He became so disfigured that even his visiting friends 'could hardly recognize him; they began to weep aloud, and they tore their robes and sprinkled dust on their heads. Then they sat on the ground with him for seven days and seven nights. No one said a word to him, because they saw how great his suffering was' (2:12-13).

Each of these two stages is terrible in itself. Severe grief is devastating to the healthiest person. And it is easier to cope with bad health while we have the love and support of our family around us. But when we join them both together — severe grief and incredible bodily affliction — we see the depths of suffering Job was going through!

And then there is his wife. As a final blow, even her sympathy and support seems to be gone. 'His wife said to him, "Are you still holding on to your integrity? Curse God and die!"' (2:9). Wrong as she was, we should be wary of overstating the case against her. True, she spoke wrongly, but too many Christians have smeared her reputation beyond the biblical context. It has been said that she is destitute of piety, and that she had no love or sympathy for her husband. It has even been alleged that Satan showed his hostility to Job not only in killing his children but in sparing his wife to torment him. Augustine labelled her '*diabolos adjutrix*' (devil's advocate). Chrysostom called her 'the devil's best scourge', and Calvin described her as '*Organum Satani*' (the embodiment of Satan).

There is no reason to assume she had been anything but a good wife to Job. The only other reference to her (19:17) is consistent with that. We would be closer to the truth to see her as a worthy companion of this godly man, approving and sharing his trust in God. At the end of the book, when Job's fortunes are restored, there is not the slightest hint that he had a new wife or that she was a dark spot on the scene. So far as the record shows, she bore the first blow as well as Job did. We hear no murmur from her lips when her ten children were taken. She seems to agree with Job's confession of faith. But now, her last earthly prop is breaking. Her beloved husband is perishing before her. The sight of him is an intolerable distress. She is well nigh frantic in despair and her fortitude gives way. Faith wavers under such dark clouds. In her distressed state she no longer thinks rationally, so she suggests foolishly that Job might as well hasten death. *Curse God and die!* Her reasoning seems to be that death will bring the relief she desires for him or, if faith in God has brought this agony, it is time for Job to reconsider his religious convictions. Surely he cannot be worse off!

We need to remember that a little later Job himself speaks foolishly and self-righteously, seeing no point in loving God. We do not write him off, so we should not treat his wife differently for any failure here on her part. Moreover, Job knew her better than all the commentators, and his reply to her does not support the harsh view. Though his reply is firm, it is not harsh. He does not say she is a fool (or evil). He does not call her 'foolish woman'. His reply was: 'You are talking like a foolish woman. Shall we accept good from God, and not trouble?' (2:10). The implication is that she is not normally like that. She is normally a wise woman, but now, because of the depressing extremity of the hour, she is acting out of character, most unlike herself!

Which one of us has not done that! Does that make us valid targets for the sharp pens of scholars? Does that make us a 'devil incarnate', or an 'embodiment of Satan'? No! Notice how Job woos her to think rationally: 'Shall we accept good from God and not trouble?' It is not her character he corrects, but her 'out of character'. He corrects not her nature, but her words. Be careful not to accuse people slanderously where Scripture does not. If we speak harshly of Job's wife, we will find him disagreeing with us. We will only put more hurt upon him, when his pain is enormous already.

Stage 3: Here the suffering is prolonged and persistent. A strong fortress can endure the early attacks, only to fall after a slow and steady siege. Constant dripping wears the hardest rock away. So Satan, having twice failed in his severe assaults on Job, no doubt feels confident that he will wear Job out by maintaining the pressure.

No longer is it the sheer amount of pain (enormous in itself) but the jeering, haunting continuity of it. The sufferer is worn and weary, his strength is drying up, his spirit is sinking, and his hope is fleeing. There is no way to calm the nerves when the hours become days and the days turn to weeks, and every moment drags heavily. Night after tedious night he watches for dawn, but it brings no relief. Day after terrible day he sighs for the cover of darkness, but it brings no rest. We will return to this theme later. It takes up most of the book, and stage three soon gets worse as the devil takes up new instruments of torture. How would you cope in this situation? So assess Job properly! Let's see how he responded.

2. Job's godly response

'Job got up and tore his robe and shaved his head. Then he fell to the ground in worship and said, "Naked I came from my mother's womb, and naked I shall depart. The LORD gave and the LORD has taken away; may the name of the LORD be praised." In all this, Job did not sin by charging God with wrongdoing' (1:20-22).

Why did Job fall to the ground, clothed with the emblems of grief and humiliation? Was it to sit in sullen silence? Was it to brood despondently? That would be understandable, but no, that was not the case. And it was not to complain and murmur 'Why me?' Job fell down as he worshipped God, blessing the name of the

Lord. It was to honour and adore the God who allowed his pain. That's what surprises us. That is so unique, so extraordinary, and so profound!

His only language is that of godly adoration. He confesses that God has every right to remove the things he had previously given. Job's theme is 'God owes me nothing—I owe him all!' 'Naked I came, blessed be the name of Jehovah!' Can humble, trustful piety reach any higher point in fallen man than this? I doubt it! Is our hardship even half as severe as Job's? I doubt it. Is our love for God even half as strong as Job's? I doubt it! What a kick in the teeth for Satan! His hatred has backfired. It was supposed to make Job curse God; instead it made him worship.

Notice too that Job's mindset is not mechanistic or deistic. He is not merely 'yielding to the inevitable and accepting fate'. Nor does he simply bow to the omnipotence of God, thinking that there is no sense resisting infinite power, no sense opposing, or questioning, or even disliking it; there is no sense in a mere creature resisting the Creator. Nor does Job merely recognize that God is right in whatever he does, whether he creates or destroys, gives or takes, supplies or withdraws.

No, Job goes way beyond all that. He actually marvels at God's goodness, a goodness that is measured and felt, strangely enough, when the good things are taken away! 'The LORD gave and the LORD has taken away; may the name of the LORD be praised.' In the words of a popular song, 'You don't know what you've got till it's gone', and the sense of loss is Job's very motive for praising God that he ever had it in the first place! It is only when we are destitute of the mercies that we daily take for granted that we realize how good God has always been to us! So this godly man does not mainly lament his loss. He worships his God. He gives thanks that he ever had things to lose in the first place! Again, what a huge blow to Satan! He wanted to prove Job was selfish, but he only proved that Job was selfless. He wanted to prove Job was 'self centred', but now it is obvious that he is 'God centred'.

Conclusions

We can all draw strength from Job. All of us suffer pain and loss and troubles of various sorts. We too can find our bright sunny day suddenly invaded by dark storms. We too can go out happy in the morning and come in broken at night.

Some of you may face trials even now. Some of you are probably in deep waters. You have fears and burdens and hurts, deep hurts. You fear for a loved one. You tremble because of an enemy. Learn from Job. He blazed a trail for us. See the hand of God in everything. See the mercies of God even when he takes them away! Remember, he does not take them away capriciously, cruelly, foolishly, or resentfully. You may not even know why he took them away, like Job. Remember that they belong to God. He gives, he takes, and he is still worthy of praise.

Job's example will sustain you, and the ultimate outcome is far better than you can imagine. We have the example of one even greater than Job. A greater sufferer has come. He lost much more than Job — he is Jesus Christ our Saviour. Do you want to honour God? Then follow Job, the Old Testament *type* of Christ. Do you want to resist Satan so that he flees? Then follow Job and Jesus. It was Jesus who, even more than Job, 'entrusted himself to him who judges justly' (1 Peter 2:23).

DISCUSS IT

QUESTIONS FOR DISCUSSION

1. *How does Romans 8:18-25 refute the claim that it is not God's will for believers to suffer?*

2. *How do Romans 5:3-5 and James 1:2-4 equip us for suffering?*

3. *Read Hebrews 12:4-12 and Psalm 119:67 & 71. Is it possible that our suffering could be a blessing in disguise?*

CHAPTER FIVE

WHO NEEDS ENEMIES?

LOOK IT UP

BIBLE READING

Job 4 - 27

INTRODUCTION

After listening to the three counsellors it is hard to avoid some antagonism. The old saying comes to mind: 'Who needs enemies with friends like that?' Job's version of it is found in his exasperated cry: 'Miserable comforters are you all! Will your long-winded speeches never end? What ails you that you keep on arguing?' (16:2-3). Who needs enemies?

Our task is to assess Job's friends. From a careful examination of each of their speeches, what impression is gained? What is the broad view, the big picture? These dialogues (chapters 4 – 27) form the largest section in the book, so it is important that we understand their context. Eliphaz, Bildad and Zophar have travelled to be with their friend in his distress. They want to comfort him and advise him of what can be done to end his agonies, so that he might return to days of peace and joy. There are three cycles of speeches; each man speaks in turn, and always in the same order (Eliphaz, then Bildad, then

Zophar). Job answers after each speech. Zophar does not speak in the third cycle.

Each man has his own way of arguing that Job has brought these sufferings upon himself. They begin with lapsed humanity, saying Job, like all men, is affected by sin: 'Yet man is born to trouble as surely as sparks fly upward' (5:7). Since God is holy and just, he would not allow suffering to fall on an undeserving person, therefore Job must deserve it. Job has sin that needs confessing and then God will restore favour and blessing.

This reasoning, though plausible, is wrong. It refutes the very heart of the gospel. It is anti-gospel reasoning because the gospel says God *does* afflict an undeserving person. A righteous person *did* suffer terribly though he was sinless. It is imperative that we come to grips with this large section in Job. We need to assess it not only through Old Testament eyes, but also from the New Testament perspective. Job typifies Christ, a man who suffered terribly but not because of personal sins, that God might destroy the works of the devil through him. Failure to recognize this means we will miss the function of the book of Job in Scripture, placing us on the way to moralizing the message. As we assess Job's friends, we can arrange our observations systematically:

1. The men
2. The message
3. The mistake

1. The men

They are not bad men. For all their faults, they are still true friends of Job. Of all who heard about Job's calamity, they are the ones who came and visited him! They sympathized deeply and mourned silently with him for seven days. They truly entered into his grief and misery, moved and shaken by the burdens of their friend. This must have helped Job. They did not advise him to 'curse God and die' like his wife did! They had the courage to confront Job face to face, not to whisper behind his back.

They are well grounded in theological truths, consistently defending the honour of God and his sovereign rights. They will not tolerate a slur upon God's name. If there is any curse or pain or anguish in this world, they will not tolerate God being imputed with fault. These are very good attributes! If only more men had such courage! They were not so soppy and sentimental as to overlook the foolish speeches of a sick man. No! Sick, or not sick, when Job casts a shadow over God's reputation and over God's handling of the universe, he must be warned! And we agree with them.

Moreover, these men were not rash young 'whipper-snappers', fresh out of school. It seems that they were venerable men with plenty of age, wisdom and experience, who spoke for many other credible people. So they claimed: 'The grey-haired and the aged are on our side, men even older than your father' (15:10). They came from countries known for their wisdom. Eliphaz, the primary speaker, is a Temanite. Teman was famous for wisdom. Much later, Jeremiah the prophet refers to it: 'Is there no longer wisdom in Teman? Has counsel perished from the prudent?' (Jeremiah 49:7).

It is crucial for the interpretation of this book that we realize these three are good men. We can all cope more readily with the criticisms of fools. The chatter of ignorant, unlearned, unwise and unspiritual men is a nuisance, but we expect that. They could never appreciate the deep issues of life. That requires a degree of refinement, nobleness of mind, wisdom, discrimination, sensitivity, breadth of knowledge and analytical thinking. Because we do not expect ignorant men to understand, we (like Job) can endure such criticism. But when it comes from solid, wise and godly men (like Eliphaz, Bildad and Zophar) it is hard to bear. When men of integrity find fault with us it cannot be dismissed lightly. When sensitive, caring, spiritual men aim their darts, it is very painful, especially when they are wrong! Who needs enemies?

2. The message

We should notice three features about the message these men presented to Job.

1. The crux of it

The crux of their case amounts to this: either Job is bad or God is bad. Job is driven into a corner. Essentially, they say repeatedly that God is good, and righteous, and fair as he controls everything in the universe! So far, so good. Job agrees. We live in a 'cause-effect' world. Suffering is caused by sin. All men are sinners. All men contribute to the suffering of the world. Sin leads to suffering and woe, while righteousness leads to blessing, mercy and peace. Again, Job is in full agreement. Then comes their conclusion. Since God is good and fair, rewarding obedience and punishing disobedience, and since he would never bless the wicked or cause the righteous to suffer, therefore Job must make a choice. There are only two alternatives to explain his frightful sufferings: bad Job or bad God!

His friends say the former is correct! He must have sinned in some way, either wittingly or unwittingly. He must have drawn the anger of God upon himself. That is what the three of them believe. So he should repent and be spared further pain. By rejecting their counsel he is maintaining his innocence at the expense of God. He must then blame God, and call God unjust for his relentless and terrible affliction on an innocent man like Job. And since that is blasphemy, and Job would not want to do that, surely he can see that their advice to him is correct. Their case is watertight.

The problem is, Job knows that neither of those alternatives is true! Job blesses God as good while he also holds to his own integrity. He does not believe his suffering is due to any fault in God or himself! And he is right. God says so! Job knew their reasoning was wrong somewhere. He knew that while much of what they said was true, there must be something missing. There must be some other explanation. Job did not know what it was, but he knew what it was not. He knew it was not simply a choice of 'bad God' or 'bad Job'. But they continued relentlessly pressing those two alternatives onto him. They thought they had a watertight theological system with each 'i' dotted, and 't' crossed, and no loose ends or gaps. And the frightening thing is that it is so plausible, so attractive, so simple, and so common in the 'fundamentalism' that pervades much of modern 'evangelicalism'.

No wonder Job protested. Leave me alone! Your counselling only makes me feel worse! Miserable comforters are you all! 'My spirit is broken ... mockers surround me; my eyes must dwell on their hostility... You have closed their minds to understanding' (17:1-4). Who needs enemies?

2. The development of it

Their speeches move from being gentle to harsh. They finish up making outrageous accusations against Job, but they certainly did not start that way. They felt driven to it because Job was not giving ground. As they saw it, he was becoming more obdurate and incorrigible. He refused to accept either end of their polemic (bad God or bad Job).

Let us recall some of the progress. After silence for seven days, Eliphaz opened the discussion in reply to Job's sad lament that he was ever born (chapter 3). It is a fairly mild address and quite elegant in places. Essentially, Eliphaz said, 'Job, you have strengthened others when they were afflicted, so don't collapse yourself! Anyway, the source of your troubles is the same for all of us. We all sin. We all share in trouble: "Man is born to trouble as surely as sparks fly upward" (5:7). The best advice is to accept it graciously and submit humbly. You are being chastened and disciplined by God. Remember, "Blessed is the man whom God corrects; so do not despise the discipline of the Almighty"' (5:17).

The trouble in Job's mind is that, as gentle as Eliphaz is, he is wrong. He assumes God is correcting Job for some sin, but Job knows it is not so (and the reader is even more certain of it). So Eliphaz is gentle but irrelevant.

Bildad turned up the heat with the cruel remark that Job's children got exactly what they deserved. They had sinned so they were destroyed. 'When your children sinned against him, [God] gave them over to the penalty of their sin' (8:4).

Shortly after, Zophar inflamed matters further, accusing Job of idleness, mockery and godless talk. 'Zophar the Naamathite replied: "Are all these words to go unanswered? Is this talker to be vindicated? Will your idle talk reduce men to silence? Will no one rebuke you when you mock? You say to God, 'My beliefs are flawless and I am pure in your sight.' Oh, how I wish that God would speak, that he would open his lips against you"' (11:1-5).

Clearly, the gentle approach to counselling was over. Zophar pressed Bildad's point more blatantly. He told Job in effect, 'God exacts from you less than your iniquity deserves' (11:6, NKJV). In other words, 'You may be suffering Job, but not half as much as you deserve!' Some bedside manner! The NIV translates it as: 'God has even forgotten some of your sin.' Zophar's implied barb is: 'What if God made you suffer for all of your sins? You are actually well-off, Job, so be thankful!' Now the gloves are off! Zophar openly accused Job of sin: 'Put away the sin that is in your hand' (11:14). The dialogue was degenerating rapidly.

As a bare theological principle, this is incontestable. Job does not dispute it. God is kind and does not treat any of us as severely as we deserve. But it is irrelevant here. Why? Because it does not explain why Job the sinner is suffering, while his fellow sinners (Eliphaz, Bildad and Zophar) are not. Job could retort with: 'Why has God apparently forgotten only some of my sins, but all of yours?' The sinfulness of all men is a true doctrine, but it cannot explain why *one* man is singled out for extraordinary suffering above all others. And Job is right — again!

The second speech from Eliphaz is much more cutting than his first. His earlier caution is gone. Job is accused of impiety, and of hindering others in their walk with God. Eliphaz argues that even if there was no previous sin to cause his suffering, there certainly is plenty of sin now, especially in Job's speeches. 'But you even undermine piety and hinder devotion to God. Your sin prompts your mouth; you adopt the tongue of the crafty. Your own mouth condemns you, not mine; your own lips testify against you' (15:4-6).

His third speech is very provocative. Eliphaz openly charged Job with the most atrocious sins: 'Is not your wickedness great? Are not your sins endless?' (22:5).

We need to pause here. What a horrible spectacle! Here is the best man on earth, whom God declares to be 'blameless and upright, a man who fears God and shuns evil' (1:8); and here are three true friends, good men, wise, lovers of God and defenders of the truth. Yet they have no scruples in openly alleging the most inhuman and ungodly iniquities of Job. Worse, it is all mere supposition, without the slightest foundation of fact. It is the fruit of theology gone wrong. It is all based on inference and filling in details where divine revelation gives no warrant to do so. We can all be guilty of the same thing if we do not learn from this!

3. The mysticism of it

When all else fails, try mysticism! Try appealing to a mystical encounter with God, which no one can prove or disprove. Try surprising them with 'a vision', 'a word from God specially given to me to pass on to you', 'a message, a revelation', outside the objective written Word of God, with no witnesses except me! Hit them with the 'super-revelation' sent down from heaven just especially for you (the audience) via me (the prophet). Claim the high spiritual ground! That is exactly what Eliphaz does.

> 'A word was secretly brought to me, my ears caught a whisper of it. Amid disquieting dreams in the night, when deep sleep falls on men, fear and trembling seized me and made all my bones shake. A spirit glided past my face, and the hair on my body stood on end. It stopped, but I could not tell what it was. A form stood before my eyes, and I heard a hushed voice: "Can a mortal be more righteous than God? Can a man be more pure than his Maker? If God places no trust in his servants, if he charges his angels with error, how much more those who live in houses of clay, whose foundations are in the dust, who are crushed more readily than a moth!"' (4:12-19).

In summary, it is allegedly a word 'from God' saying, 'Job is in error. If God even finds error in the angels, how much more will he find it in those, like Job, who live in houses of clay? So own up Job!' But this whole thing is *utter nonsense*! God did not give Eliphaz any such vision! God later rebuked Eliphaz for his speech (42:7).

I do not propose to explain how Eliphaz got this silly idea into his head. I do not even insist it was a deliberate lie. It could have been a hunch, a dream, or a strong and well-motivated wish to change Job. Or it could have been a nightmare, a delusion, or even a satanic suggestion. Who knows, and what docs it matter? What I do insist is that it is very arrogant and very dangerous, yet it is lamentably very common even today. Whenever I hear a speech begin with: 'God told me'; 'God has placed this message, this burden, this word on my heart'; a real shudder goes down my spine. It is mystical, extra-biblical, and certainly not verifiable. It is thoroughly out of bounds for Christians.

What God *has* told me can be verified, because he has told you and everyone else the same thing. It is in Scripture. Once you go beyond Scripture for your theology or for counselling, you have left orthodox faith. You have gone into mysticism, into subjectivism, and the unseen and unverifiable experiences of hunches and feelings.

REMEMBER THIS

We ignore this truth at our peril!

> The will of God for us in every issue of life is either explicitly written in the Bible or comes from it by good and logical reasoning. The Bible is a sufficient guide for faith and life. It is well expressed in the *Westminster Shorter Catechism,* Question 2: 'What rule has God given to direct us how we may glorify and enjoy him? The Word of God, which is contained in the Scriptures of the Old and New Testaments, is *the only rule* to direct us how we may glorify and enjoy him.'

A good dose of church history would satisfy anyone who doubts this assertion, providing voluminous evidence of the folly of subjectivism in every age! And here it is in one of the most ancient Old Testament books. There is no point saying, 'But God used it and blessed it in my experience.' Yes, God is so marvellous he even uses human folly to bless his people. But that is all credit to his grace and no credit to our stupidity. God used a donkey to teach a mistaken prophet which way to go (Numbers 22:21-35). Shall we employ more donkeys?

3. The mistake

We shall consider more of their speeches when we look at Job's famous poem on wisdom (see chapter 8), but the errors of his three friends are already evident. Their mistake arose not from any of the parts of their theology, but from their mechanistic abuse of it. Their creed was essentially correct. God is good and just and sovereign. God is on the side of the righteous but he opposes the wicked. All men are sinners. All deserve suffering. No one suffers as much as he deserves. Yes, it is a 'cause-effect' world, a world of order, reliability and predictability. 'Amen' to all of that. But this true theology is incomplete. It cannot answer every question. Even now, with the full canon of sixty-six books, human knowledge remains deficient.

There are gaps in our knowledge. There are problems which man cannot solve and which the Bible makes no attempt to answer. There is a 'secret will' of God, a secret counsel, an unrevealed purpose (Deuteronomy 29:29) and we must allow for that. God had a purpose in afflicting Job but that purpose was not revealed in those days. Indeed it was not revealed until Christ came. Let me explain. According to the excellent 'systematic theology' of the day (in which Eliphaz, Bildad and Zophar were all extremely well qualified), suffering could be explained in two ways. Either it was *justice* (punishment for sin) or it was *sanctification* (refining from sin). Evidence for the first is plentiful, including Noah's flood, Sodom's burning, and

Pharaoh's plagues. Evidence for the second is also clear (Hebrews 12). But neither of them explains Job's case.

Why did Job suffer? The answer lies in a feature of biblical literature known as *typology*. A 'type' is a person (like Moses) or event (like the Exodus) or institution (like the Passover) that recurs in the person and work of Christ. A 'type' is a preview of an even greater Messianic reality (*antitype*). As a true 'type', Job provides a historic preview of Christ. Job is a shadow of Christ. Job is an innocent man who suffers terribly, out of all proportion. He suffered not because he justly deserved it, and not in order to refine and improve him, but as God's instrument against Satan. In Job and Jesus, God uses the anguish of his chosen innocent man to frustrate and defeat the malicious plans of Satan. The ultimate purpose of the book of Job is quite unclear until the New Testament. Lines drawn in Job finally converge upon Christ. The book of Job cannot be understood from the Old Testament alone.

Typology is an important tool.

In the world of computers, a True Type is a scaleable printing font. It has a standard (default) form with its own size, shape and proportion. But it can be reproduced in an enlarged or scaled-up form, without any distortion.

THINK ABOUT IT

In the world of biblical studies, a True Type is a scaleable person, event, or institution. It is first seen (default mode) in its original historical setting, with its own meaning in that original environment. But God scales it up later on, meaning he causes the type to be expanded so that it stretches beyond its original (default) setting but without loss of proportion. The original person, event, or thing is repeated in some larger form in connection with Christ and his kingdom.

Typology opens up marvellous insights into the Old Testament, but care is needed. Not all the Old Testament is typological, to be enlarged beyond its original setting. There are 'rules'. There must be a significant (not trivial) resemblance between type and antitype, and the point of resemblance must be intended by God (natural and unforced), not merely accidental, coincidental, plausible, or contrived.

Indeed, God himself becomes the innocent sufferer at Calvary! The anguish of Job is an insight into how God feels about the cross. The counsel of Job's three well-meaning friends is an insight into the advice Jesus received from his friends. They also urged him to cease his course of pain. 'Never, Lord! This shall never happen to you!' (Matthew 16:22). His response indicated the real source of the trouble: 'Get behind me, Satan.'

The wisdom of the gospel seems foolish to the world. But it is higher than our ways. Let us learn not to presume we can explain all suffering. We can explain some suffering, but we must say no more than Scripture allows. We must leave room for the secret will of God. Trust him and advise others likewise. Had Job's counsellors simply admitted: 'There are gaps in our knowledge, we cannot explain, but we will support you and comfort you,' they would have been much more help.

QUESTIONS FOR DISCUSSION

1. *Read Matthew 24:36-39 where Noah's flood is compared to Christ's return. Exactly how is the flood a 'type', i.e. what is the intended point of resemblance between the two events?*

2. *Paul openly describes Adam as a 'type' of Christ in Romans 5:14. Read that chapter. What is the intended 'typical' connection between Adam and Christ?*

3. *Read Deuteronomy 29:29; Psalm 19:7-14; Psalm 119:96-105; and 2 Timothy 3:14-17. What are they telling us about knowing the will of God in daily life?*

CHAPTER SIX

IS GOD TRUSTWORTHY?

LOOK IT UP

BIBLE READING

Job 1:6-22

INTRODUCTION

This question announces a major theme in the Bible's events, characters and crises. Its importance in the book of Job is best appreciated when we see it in its larger biblical context. Simply put, the question is this: 'Can God be trusted just because he is God?' When God speaks his mind, is that enough? Is his bare word sufficient ground for our wholehearted loyalty, obedience and trust, even if he only briefly commands our duty with no explanation, explication or example? Is God plus nothing sufficient? Is God minus everything adequate grounds for trusting him? Do I need to have all the 'hows', 'whys', 'ifs', 'buts', 'wherefores', and 'therefores' clarified, or even just some of them? Is it enough that God has spoken? Is knowledge of God sufficient for faith or do I need knowledge about knowledge? Is God trustworthy standing all alone by himself, or is he only trustworthy when we can see him with all the circumstances, facts and assurances involved?

The answer of course is that God is a sufficient basis for our loyalty: God in isolation, God plus nothing. God minus everything is more than enough reason for trust on our part. There is no valid excuse for doubting God. Notwithstanding the curiosity and weakness of man, our unanswerable questions, the gaps in our knowledge, and the endless pursuit of unrevealed things while ignoring the revealed things, God is wholly trustworthy.

Almighty God is, in himself, the *immense imperative*. He is the ultimate reason that swamps and overwhelms all our 'whys', and 'wherefores' and 'ifs' and 'buts'. The God who inhabits eternity is the unanswerable response to our little time-bound problems. The Lord who knows all things, causing everything to achieve his purposes, is an awesome response to all our puny questions.

The burden of Scripture and gospel is that all men must come to trust him sincerely. We must completely abandon ourselves to God. We must trust him simply because he is God. That is what pleases God. That is what honours God and crushes Satan. That is what mature Christianity is all about. There will be times when all the supports of reason and experience will fail us. Our logic and theological acumen will provide no answer. Then we will see if we really find God trustworthy. It is variously worded in Scripture: 'Be still, and know that I am God'; 'God is our refuge and strength'; 'Let God be true, and every man a liar' (Psalm 46:10; Psalm 46:1; Romans 3:4). The importance of this issue is illustrated in the lives of characters like Noah, Abraham, Joshua and Daniel. We will now explore whether God is trustworthy:

1. For Adam and Eve
2. For Job
3. For Jesus

1. For Adam and Eve

'You are free to eat from any tree in the garden; but you must not eat from the tree of the knowledge of good and evil, for when you eat of it you will surely die' (Genesis 2:16-17).

There it was, the bare word of God in man's probationary test. It amounts to one issue: 'Is God trustworthy?' This whole event has raised theological eyebrows. Why have this test? If God desires the supreme happiness of man, why risk human ruin and death by setting up this test? Why not rule out any possibility of sin occurring? Part of the answer recognizes that virtue involves choices. Ethical-religious behaviour is where a choice needs to be made. To do what God wants under compulsion, where no possibility of doing wrong exists, has no moral, rational, ethical or religious worth. It has no spiritual value, no virtue. But man is a moral-spiritual creature made in the image of God, so there had to be a choice, a test.

This is true enough but inadequate. The probation in Eden reveals the Creator. The initiative for it and all its terms and conditions were his. It was designed to show that God is trustworthy even when there is nothing else around to prove it. The tree of knowledge was just one of the many trees God had made. It was perfectly good and perfectly harmless like the rest. It had good fruit. There was nothing sinister or magical about it (as the serpent suggested). So, it was an arbitrary tree. Any other tree in the garden could have served the same purpose. God did not have to pick this exact tree, the one next to it would have done. The command to abstain from it was a 'positive law', meaning there was nothing intrinsically harmful about that tree. If God had not forbidden it, it was perfectly proper for mankind to eat from it. So the probationary command to Adam and Eve meant: 'Eat from all the other trees, but not from this equally good tree.' The bottom line for Adam and Eve is: Shall God be trusted just because he is God? Is his bare word sufficient for me? Is God trustworthy?

They faced a choice where human reason cannot guide. Investigation would be impossible. There did not appear to be any moral, scientific or pragmatic reason for abstaining from the fruit. If they had analysed it chemically, it would have proven healthy. It was a good wholesome diet! So why did God forbid it? No reason was given! Curiosity remains curious; paradox remains paradox; mystery remains mystery. The only thing perfectly clear is that God said, 'Don't'. There is no reason to obey except that God says so. Even the concept of 'death' was outside their experience. There is no reason to fear death except for God's warning! Is God trustworthy?

Adam and Eve failed. They presumed that God needs character references before he can be trusted. They presumed that God is not trustworthy by himself. They acted as though the bare word of God is insufficient. They implied that godliness must wait for human curiosity to be satisfied first, by empirical research. God's word must be judged at the bar of scientific method and experimentation. So, the first science experiment in human history was conducted. Eden became a laboratory. The godless logic of Professor Serpent suggested that knowledge has to be based upon experience. The sure way to know is to eat it and see. Depending on the results, we will find out if God is trustworthy and reliable after all! They presumed to put God on probation.

The tempter seemed to know his subject well. He interpreted the tree as a 'taboo tree' or 'magic tree'. His sinister speech implies that it was a problematic part of God's creation. God has some real fears about this tree. He fears he has created a 'monster' because anyone who eats of it will become just like him, equal with God, but God cannot stand competition. So he is envious, and scared, and that is why he is trying to terrify you with these silly threats of death! But no, you will not die! Do not just take God's word for it! Yes, we know what God said. But he has not said enough! It is what he has not said that really counts. So seek after knowledge. *Savoir c'est pouvoir* (knowledge is power). Plot your own course. God's motives look quite different in the light of all the evidence he has kept back. So go on, gather in the evidence and you will see that he is not trustworthy.

But it was all lies from the father of lies. They found out the hard way that God *is* reliable. So much for 'Act 1' in that historic motif.

2. For Job

There is not the slightest doubt that Job saw God as absolutely trustworthy. Who can ever forget his heroic confession against terrible odds: 'The Lord gave and the Lord has taken away; may the name of the Lord be praised' (1:21). That is how Job emerged from the first satanic onslaught. And who can doubt his faith as he emerges from the second terrible blow: 'Shall we accept good from God, and not trouble?' (2:10). Of course God is trustworthy, even God plus troubles.

But in the prolonged third stage of his sufferings Job was pushed to the limit on this question. Paradoxically, his troubles were aggravated because of his faith in God. Satan worked overtime to prove the opposite thesis that God is only trustworthy when things go well. God only has Job's love when Job can see good reasons for it. But take away those reasons, remove those props and supports, and watch Job curse God. Watch Job conclude that God is not trustworthy. '"Does Job fear God for nothing?" Satan replied. "Have you not put a hedge around him and his household and everything he has? You have blessed the work of his hands, so that his flocks and herds are spread throughout the land. But stretch out your hand and strike everything he has, and he will surely curse you to your face"' (1:9-11).

So, for a moment, let us enter into Job's anguish. To begin with, Job had no doubts at all that God was in control of even this miserable situation. Job said, 'His wisdom is profound, his power is vast. Who has resisted him and come out unscathed?' (9:4-5). How vigorously Job made that point: 'But ask the animals, and they will teach you, or the birds of the air, and they will tell you; or speak to the earth, and it will teach you, or let the fish of the sea inform you. Which of all these does not know that the hand of the LORD has done this? In his hand is the life of every creature and the breath of all mankind' (12:7-10). Job knows God has purposed and permitted these agonies to come upon him, though the reason is unknown to Job. But that is precisely the problem! He knows God is in control of these agonies and yet God has not said why! Job's mind is confronted with the reality of God alone, God plus nothing, and we see him really struggling.

> 'I loathe my very life; therefore I will give free rein to my complaint and speak out in

the bitterness of my soul. I will say to God: Do not condemn me, but tell me what charges you have against me. Does it please you to oppress me, to spurn the work of your hands, while you smile on the schemes of the wicked? Do you have eyes of flesh? Do you see as a mortal sees? Are your days like those of a mortal or your years like those of a man, that you must search out my faults and probe after my sin — though you know that I am not guilty and that no one can rescue me from your hand? Your hands shaped me and made me. Will you now turn and destroy me? Remember that you moulded me like clay. Will you now turn me to dust again? Did you not pour me out like milk and curdle me like cheese, clothe me with skin and flesh and knit me together with bones and sinews?

'You gave me life and showed me kindness, and in your providence watched over my spirit. But this is what you concealed in your heart, and I know that this was in your mind: If I sinned, you would be watching me and would not let my offence go unpunished. If I am guilty — woe to me! Even if I am innocent, I cannot lift my head, for I am full of shame and drowned in my affliction. If I hold my head high, you stalk me like a lion and again display your awesome power against me. You bring new witnesses against me and increase your anger towards me; your forces come against me wave upon wave. Why then did you bring me out of the womb? I wish I had died before any eye saw me. If only I had never come into being, or had been carried straight from the womb to the grave! Are not my few days almost over? Turn away from me so that I can have a moment's joy before I go to the place of no return, to the land of gloom and deep shadow, to the land of deepest night, of deep shadow and disorder, where even the light is like darkness' (10:1-22).

Earlier he had said, 'The arrows of the Almighty are in me, my spirit drinks in their poison; God's terrors are marshalled against me' (6:4). Job struggled to continue believing what he believed. The pressure was massive. But he realized God was his only hope. 'Oh, that I might have my request, that God would grant what I hope for, that God would be willing to crush me, to let loose his hand and cut me off! Then I would still have this consolation — my joy in unrelenting pain — that I had not denied the words of the Holy One' (6:8-10). He confesses the Holy One, yet he knows the Holy One is afflicting him. Like another distressed father, Job is really saying, 'I do believe; help me overcome my unbelief!' (Mark 9:24). I do trust, help me overcome my temptation to distrust.

Paraphrased, Job's turmoil amounts to this: 'Lord, if you were not so big and so sovereign, it would let us both off the hook! If you were not the only one pulling the strings in this universe, calling the tune, if there were other “gods” involved, I could understand. I could curse them and exonerate you, keeping my integrity. But Lord, you alone are God. The very birds of the air and fish of the sea know that; therefore you hem me in. I'm forced to come back to you, O God. Everything around me drives me from you, causing doubt and distrust. Nothing in my experience makes sense. Lord, even you don't make sense, but whom else can I go to? I want to find you trustworthy, but I'm sinking, Lord!'

If ever a mere man was faced with God alone, it is Job. There is nothing left, no one to turn to, only God: God plus nothing, God minus everything. Job would have had no trouble singing Edward Mote's hymn:

When all around my soul gives way
He then is all my hope and stay.
When darkness seems to veil his face
I rest on his unchanging grace.[1]

It is good to marvel at Job's triumphant faith. The Bible commends him as an example to encourage us (James 5:11). Yes, God is trustworthy. ‘Though he slay me, yet will I hope in him’ (Job 13:15). Job stood firm: ‘Even now my witness is in heaven; my advocate is on high’ (16:19). Job's faith saw beyond the clouds: ‘I know that my Redeemer lives, and that in the end he will stand upon the earth. And after my skin has been

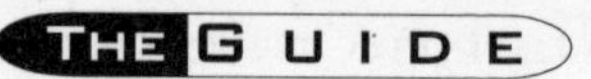

destroyed, yet in my flesh I will see God; I myself will see him with my own eyes — I, and not another. How my heart yearns within me!' (19:25-27).

3. For Jesus

In the horrors of Golgotha we see the supreme evidence that God is trustworthy. Here was a greater man than Job. Jesus was 'holy, blameless, pure, set apart from sinners' (Hebrews 7:26). Here was a purer faith than Job's, and a hotter furnace to try it. Whereas Job's troubles hit him suddenly and unexpectedly, Jesus knew about his trials long beforehand. In Gethsemane Jesus was already feeling the crucifixion before it happened. He was sweating drops like blood. His soul was grieved unto death. 'He offered up prayers and petitions with loud cries and tears to the one who could save him from death' (Hebrews 5:7).

Whereas Job longed to die, ending his sufferings, Jesus asked to avoid the death before him because it climaxed his sufferings. 'Father, everything is possible for you. Take this cup from me' (Mark 14:36). In other words, 'Father, you agree I'm innocent, so I'm not asking something unreasonable. Why should I be cursed? Why should I go through hell? Why should I be judged for sin?' So Jesus was left with nothing but God!

Here again is the historic theme: *Is God trustworthy?* Is he trustworthy in death, even an undeserved and violent death? Can God be trusted when violent men are free to do their worst? Is trusting God the Father made odious by the murder of his Son?

There's something profound here.

Of course Jesus knew the answer to his 'Why?' question: 'My God, why have you forsaken me?' For three years he had been teaching his disciples why he came to die. 'Now my heart is troubled, and what shall I say? "Father, save me from this hour"? No, it was for this very reason I came to this hour' (John 12:27). His 'Why?' was not seeking information. Rather, it alerts us to the unspeakable horrors of divine judgement. Christ knew he would bear the pains of hell for the salvation of his people. But no amount of knowledge can prepare a man for the experience of judgement for sin. No words can describe the unspeakable reality of retribution and rejection by God. Knowing about hell is one thing; enduring it is quite another.

So, when there are no answers forthcoming, when a man's commitment to God alone says, 'Yet not my will, but yours be done' (Luke 22:42), and when friendly reasoning left to itself protests, 'Never, Lord! This shall never happen to you!' (Matthew 16:22), what does Jesus do? 'He entrusted himself to him who judges justly' (1 Peter 2:23).

The staggering thing is that even when God has left him, Jesus still trusts God! When God has judicially abandoned him and turned his face away, that is the moment of trust and commitment: 'Into your hands I commit my spirit' (Luke 23:46). God is trustworthy! God plus nothing! God minus everything! God withdrawn! He is trustworthy when he afflicts, abandons and crushes, no less than when he comforts, draws near and blesses.

God remains good, just, wise and holy at all moments. He cannot be anything else. If he tests us, like Adam and Eve, he is trustworthy. If he keeps silent about the details, he is trustworthy. If he afflicts us, he remains trustworthy and has good purposes. If he abandons even the choicest of his servants (Job, Jesus), he remains trustworthy and cannot deny himself.

How commendable it is to trust God. How hopeless, futile and soul-destroying it is to doubt him. Have you come to the point of sincere trust in God? Is your confidence in him alone? If God removes everything else that comforts you, is *he* your comfort? Life will bring us face to face with this issue more than once. May our answer be consistent with that of Christ: 'Into your hands I commit my spirit.'

Questions for Discussion

1. *What important truths about the trustworthiness of God are found in James 1:13-17?*

2. *God is not the author of evil though he purposed it. How do Ecclesiastes 7:29; Proverbs 16:4; Isaiah 55:9; and Jude 6 help us deal with the origin of evil?*

3. *'I have more insight than all my teachers, for I meditate on your statutes' (Psalm 119:99). Is that arrogant? Adam sinned because he stopped believing that. Do you agree?*

CHAPTER SEVEN

THE MYSTERY OF PROVIDENCE

LOOK IT UP

BIBLE READING

Job 21

INTRODUCTION

Providence is mysterious. It refers to whatever God allows to happen as he runs the universe, whatever his sovereign purpose provides. It includes all blessings and judgements, all health and sickness, all sunshine and storms; all the expected and unexpected things. We cannot explain why they occur. We cannot know the rationale behind providence. Some things leave us with questions, not answers. It is one of the clearest lessons in the book of Job and is the main point Job made as he answered his three friends. Why did Job assert the mystery of providence?

Because his friends denied it! Their 'cause and effect' world view implied that 'problems' (like human suffering) are analogous to maths problems. They might look hard at first, but they are easily solved once you apply the right formula. In Job's case the formula they used involved the attributes of God. 'Since God is good and just and fair, and in full control of the universe, then Job must have committed some terrible sin, otherwise he would not be suffering so terribly.' We have observed how plausibly and powerfully they argued their case and how they forced Job into a corner. He must conclude that either Job is bad or God is bad.

But Job maintained his innocence. His sufferings are not due to any sin in him; and God agrees. Job accepts that God is in control, and he is not unjust, and in afflicting Job God remains good. He concludes that there must be some other explanation. There must be some facts missing in the reasoning of his three friends. Yes, and these facts concern the mysterious nature of providence. That is Job's argument in chapter 21. Essentially he says: 'Look here, Eliphaz, Bildad and Zophar. I cannot explain why I am suffering. God has not told me, and he has not told you. It is a mystery to us, but you do not like mystery! There are gaps in our knowledge but you do not like gaps! There are unanswered questions, but you manufacture answers.'

What an important lesson for us! Simplistic presumption is still a very serious danger in our day, even among well-meaning and devout people. That is why 'fundamentalist' has become a dirty word. It denotes those who reduce complex issues down to a simple, manageable, generalized formula. As a result, people are hurt by glib and sweeping conclusions. Their wounds are enlarged by the judgemental naivety of those who are confident they understand God's secret will. By no means was Job the last victim of such presumptive counsellors. To deny mystery is to deny reality. However, the mystery of providence is not uniform.

We can explain some providential happenings with a degree of confidence. It is not so mysterious when a terrorist is killed by his own bomb, or a drunk falls in front of a train, or a lazy student fails an exam. But how do we explain the tiny baby in his mother's arms also killed by the terrorist? What about the innocent passenger killed on impact with the side of the carriage when the driver braked to avoid the drunk? How do we explain the diligent, clever student who also failed an exam? Why was Sydney's brilliant surgeon, Dr Chan, killed by thugs? We cannot know. There is mystery in providence.

Why the prolonged droughts in Australia? It is embarrassing to hear simplistic Christian answers, such as: 'The drought is God's judgement on our sinful nation.' We do not deny the nation is sinful, but why do the animals suffer? They do not sin. And why are those in the rural areas singled out? Are they worse sinners than those in the cities? Is the notorious red-light district of King's Cross in Sydney, Australia (with plenty of food and water), a less sinful place than Australian country towns like Charleville or Roma after three years of drought? The drought has a minimal affect on the former but cripples the latter! Only God knows why. To us it is a mystery. It is a very practical issue. It is helpful to observe two things about the mystery in providence.

1. The mystery recognized
2. The mystery resolved

1. The mystery recognized

Job was finding it hard to get a word in edgeways. His friends were so busy talking with all their misguided confidence that he had to tell them politely to keep quiet for a minute. 'Listen carefully to my words' (21:2); 'Bear with me while I speak' (21:3); 'Clap your hand over your mouth' (21:5). The ancient Arabic proverb is good advice: 'We have two ears but one mouth so that we should listen twice as much as we speak.' It agrees with the Bible's exhortation to be slow to speak and quick to listen (James 1:19).

Having gained their attention, Job's first proof of the mystery in providence was the indisputable fact that good things happen to bad people.

The wicked prosper

> 'Why do the wicked live on, growing old and increasing in power? They see their children established around them, their offspring before their eyes. Their homes are safe and free from fear; the rod of God is not upon them. Their bulls never fail to breed; their cows calve and do not miscarry. They send forth their children as a flock; their little ones dance about. They sing to the music of

> tambourine and harp; they make merry to the sound of the flute. They spend their years in prosperity and go down to the grave in peace. Yet they say to God, "Leave us alone! We have no desire to know your ways. Who is the Almighty, that we should serve him? What would we gain by praying to him?" But their prosperity is not in their own hands, so I stand aloof from the counsel of the wicked' (21:7-16).

The wicked *do* prosper, sometimes even more than law-abiding citizens. They often outlive the godly (hence the English proverb, 'Only the good die young'). They often establish powerful dynasties (v. 8). They have homes that seem safe and free; 'the rod of God is not upon them' (v. 9): God is not punishing and cursing them — on the contrary! Everything they touch turns to gold. They get richer and richer. Their business dealings profit handsomely, 'their bulls never fail to breed — their cows calve and do not miscarry' (v. 10). They have big state funerals. They do not always die as unhappy, tormented men: 'they go down to the grave in peace' (v. 13).

To make matters worse, they not only ignore God, they openly defy him. Their irreligious mindset is arrogant. They snub their noses at God and every suggestion of judgement. 'Yet they say to God, "Leave us alone! We have no desire to know your ways. Who is the Almighty, that we should serve him?"' (vv. 14-15). They provoke God's wrath and incite his terrible vengeance. But nothing seems to happen. They live very successful, happy lives! The blessings roll on. Explain that with your simplistic theology of cause and effect!

While Job agrees with the general truth of cause and effect, his point is that there are exceptions. What explains the exceptions? And if the three friends answer, as they do, that ultimately the wicked will receive judgement in hell while the godly receive blessings in heaven, Job simply points out that this ignores the issue! He agrees with the final judgement, but why do good men suffer terribly *here and now,* while wicked men prosper in sin here and now? Why is Abel murdered in the prime of life while his killer, Cain, enjoys many more years under divine protection? So we must recognize the mystery!

A trap to avoid!

It is easy to covet and admire the prosperity of the wicked. Asaph tells how it happened to him: 'My feet had almost slipped; I had nearly lost my foothold. For I envied the arrogant when I saw the prosperity of the wicked. They have no struggles; their bodies are healthy and strong. They are free from the burdens common to man; they are not plagued by human ills' (Psalm 73:2-5).

It made him wonder if there is any point in virtue. Why bother being godly if the wicked prosper while I suffer? 'Surely in vain have I kept my heart pure; in vain have I washed my hands in innocence' (v. 13). Pragmatism was attractive. But he went on to dismiss such reasoning. Providence is fleeting and fickle. The wicked man's prosperity will not help him. It does not indicate his reality. 'Surely you place them on slippery ground; you cast them down to ruin. How suddenly are they destroyed, completely swept away by terrors!' (vv. 18-19). Beware of guidance from providence! It is a trap. Our only sure guide is the revealed will of God, that is, Scripture.

Grace creates tensions

This is Job's second proof of mystery in providence. God's grace brings unknown quantities into the equation. 'Yet how often is the lamp of the wicked snuffed out? How often does calamity come upon them, the fate God allots in his anger? How often are they like straw before the wind, like chaff swept away by a gale? It is said, "God stores up a man's punishment for his sons." Let him repay the man himself, so that he will know it! Let his own eyes see his destruction; let him drink of the wrath of the Almighty. For what does he care about the family he leaves behind when his allotted months come to an end?' (21:17-21).

God's patience towards wicked men intrudes on the principle of cause and effect. If we look at human history broadly, we rarely see God thunder out judgements as they are deserved. 'How often is the lamp of the wicked snuffed out? How often does calamity come upon them, the fate God allots in his anger?' The implied answer is 'Not often!' It is the amazing love of God and his long-suffering patience that creates 'problems' for interpreting human history. That is what creates mystery in providence. You cannot suggest that our fortunes in life are directly related to our behaviour. You cannot be simplistic like that. You cannot explain the happiness of wicked men with the formula: 'They are blessed because God is pleased with them.' Nor can you explain the troubles and afflictions of good men like Job with the presumption: 'It is because God is displeased with them!'

By definition, there are no 'rules' or 'laws' to govern mercy. Mercy is a free gift of God. It is his totally undeserved favour to men and women who deserve only wrath. Mercy comes wherever and whenever God so wills. It is totally unpredictable. 'I will have mercy on whom I have mercy, and I will have compassion on whom I have compassion' (Romans 9:15).

But then a new thought arises. What if God is kind to a wicked man in his own lifetime? Perhaps the penalty will crash down on his heirs. They may inherit his debts or his enemies or his reputation. Sooner or later his bubble will burst. Job has predicted that response too (21:19). His answer is: *So what?* What does the bad man care about the family he leaves behind? He is dead and gone. What does it do to him? Far from reducing the mystery, it makes it bigger. Why should children suffer for the sins of their fathers? When all the known principles of truth have had their say, many things in life remain unclear. Recognize the mystery in providence!

All the questions about providence ultimately get back to one issue: Why does a good God allow evil? Why does a God of love allow suffering? Why does he allow the wicked to prosper and the godly to burn at the stake? Notwithstanding the many true things that we can say, the answer is still ultimately mysterious! It belongs to the secret will of God and we dare not presume to know it. We dare not act as 'god' to our fellow men, interpreting their lives for them, explaining the providential twists and turns with a wave of the magic wand of 'cause and effect'. The last thing needed by hurting people is the voice of opinionated advisers who presume to interpret providence.

2. The mystery resolved

Notice the word is not 'solved' but 'resolved'. Nowhere does the Bible remove all mysteries from man. A mystery 'solved' is no longer a mystery. What Job shows us is how to resolve mystery, how to cope with the tensions it creates. How do we live with gaps in our thinking? How do we tread safely with black holes in our path? How do we face questions that God declines to answer? Even Job did not find it easy. Though he dismantled their 'mechanistic universe' when he taught his advisers about providence, Job also said some foolish things. He gave some unwise comments about what was happening to himself, comments he ended up regretting. How did it happen?

Paradoxically, it was resolved when God spoke out of a whirlwind *making the mystery even greater!*[1] In effect, God said to Job: 'Who do you think you are? Why do you think God is like a man? Why do you think that if men have mysteries, God does too? Why do you fret and trouble yourself with unanswered questions as if God faces the questions too? Why do you imply that if God answered, you would understand? Don't you know the vast difference between God and man? Are you capable of understanding mysteries even if I tell you? Let me show you some real mysteries.' So God interrogated Job: 'Where were you when I laid the earth's foundation? Tell me, if you understand' (38:4). What a massive question! No answer was needed and God continued:

> 'Can you bind the beautiful Pleiades? Can you loose the cords of Orion? Can you bring forth the constellations in their seasons or lead out the Bear with its cubs? Do you know the laws of the

> heavens? Can you set up God's dominion over the earth? Can you raise your voice to the clouds and cover yourself with a flood of water? Do you send the lightning bolts on their way? Do they report to you, "Here we are"? Who endowed the heart with wisdom or gave understanding to the mind? Who has the wisdom to count the clouds? Who can tip over the water jars of the heavens when the dust becomes hard and the clods of earth stick together?' (38:31-38).

How incompetent man is! How intimidating God is in his greatness! Job hears more.

> 'Can you pull in the leviathan with a fishhook or tie down his tongue with a rope? Can you put a cord through his nose or pierce his jaw with a hook? Will he keep begging you for mercy? Will he speak to you with gentle words? Will he make an agreement with you for you to take him as your slave for life? Can you make a pet of him like a bird or put him on a leash for your girls? Will traders barter for him? Will they divide him up among the merchants? Can you fill his hide with harpoons or his head with fishing spears? If you lay a hand on him, you will remember the struggle and never do it again! Any hope of subduing

> him is false; the mere sight of him is overpowering. No one is fierce enough to rouse him. Who then is able to stand against me? Who has a claim against me that I must pay? Everything under heaven belongs to me' (41:1-11).

Be still and know that I am God! God's whirlwind speeches set us back on our heels. What an immense and awesome God he is! How full of power and wisdom! Nothing can disturb the peace and serenity of his government of the cosmos. Things beyond our understanding, such as creation out of nothing, are elementary to him! Things that make us tremble, such as claps of thunder and bolts of lightning, are merely God's servants doing his bidding! He has exhaustive knowledge of the constellations and the vast distances of outer space. He rules them all with consummate ease!

The way to resolve mystery is to get a fresh insight into the immensity of God. We must listen to God's self-revelation. Let us not be intimidated by a particular mystery or an unanswered question. Rather, let us be intimidated and awestruck by the glorious God who inhabits eternity, before whom there are no puzzles, no mysteries, no anxieties and no frustrations.

Look at the profound effect it had on Job! 'Then Job answered the LORD: "I am unworthy — how can I reply to you? I put my hand over my mouth. I spoke once, but I have no answer — twice, but I will say no more"' (40:3-5). But he did say more because he was on a steep learning curve.

'Then Job replied to the LORD: "I know that you can do all things; no plan of yours can be thwarted. You asked, 'Who is this that obscures my counsel without knowledge?' Surely I spoke of things I did not understand, things too wonderful for me to know. You said, 'Listen now, and I will speak; I will question you, and you shall answer me.' My ears had heard of you but now my eyes have seen you. Therefore I despise myself and repent in dust and ashes"' (42:1-6).

Job wisely admitted he had no answer to many things. He was surrounded by mystery and so are we. God's existence is a mystery. His infinite nature is a mystery. Creation is a mystery. The resurrection is a mystery, as is the incarnation of deity in the virgin birth of Christ. The love and mercy of God are a mystery. If we deny mystery we deny the gospel. If we give slick answers to mystery we delude our neighbours and ourselves. Charles Wesley summed it up so well:

'Tis mystery all! The immortal dies!
Who can explore His strange design?
In vain the first-born seraph tries
To sound the depths of love divine.[2]

Our response should be like that of the apostle Paul: 'Oh, the depth of the riches of the wisdom and knowledge of God! How unsearchable his judgements, and his paths beyond tracing out! Who has known the mind of the Lord?' (Romans 11:33-34).

Conclusions

Firstly, God has secrets that remain secrets. Men cannot know them. They are not our business. They could only be understood by an infinite mind. We will never be infinite. We do not need to know these secret things. What God has told us in Scripture is quite sufficient to cope with them: 'The secret things belong to the LORD our God, but the things revealed belong to us and to our children for ever, that we may follow all the words of this law' (Deuteronomy 29:29). Let us take heed to what God does reveal. Do not worry about the rest!

Secondly, our view of history is analogous with our view of a giant jigsaw puzzle. It covers a large area with thousands of individual pieces. All we see is one piece here and another piece there, and while we can fit some pieces into the picture, others remain mysterious. Where does it fit? Of course it helps considerably to have the box, with a picture of the end result, and all the pieces fitted together. Even so, we'll make many wrong assumptions along the way. The Bible tells us what the end result of history will be: 'An administration suitable to the fulness of the times, that is, the summing up of all things in Christ, things in heaven and things upon the earth' (Ephesians 1:10, NASB). It is a kingdom of perfect righteousness under Christ from which all devils and all unbelieving rebels are banished. But God has not finished the process of assembling it. Thus we cannot see how some pieces fit. We still have to ask, 'Why this Hitler? Why this Bosnia? Why this plague? Why this suffering Job?'

Thirdly, while it is true that there are no mysteries or anxieties or trials or frustrations for God, we must not conclude that he is remote, or insensitive, or unsympathetic to us. On the contrary, he has drawn near in love. Our ultimate comfort is not a whole string of logical propositions to help us cope with mystery. In Christ, God has entered into our woes and miseries, taking our curse and our afflictions upon himself. The ultimate mystery is not suffering man, but suffering God!

REMEMBER THIS

Can God suffer?

The doctrine of *Impassibility* rightly denies certain forms of suffering in God. He is never dysfunctional, so he never suffers breakdown, anxiety, or neurosis. He has no paranoia, no insecurity, inadequacy, or uncertainty. God cannot lose his composure. And unlike us, God never suffers passively, against his will. He is never a helpless victim with problems just 'dumped on his plate'. God's experiences are all by his own arrangement. And God cannot suffer by losing self-control. He never explodes in a moment of pent-up emotions. He never regrets what he did. He never wishes he could turn the clock back (be careful with Genesis 6:6). He never has pangs of conscience. He has no moments of indiscretion.

But do not overdo 'Impassibility'. God is not a stone. He is not 'pure apathy'. The Bible describes a full range of emotions in God, like wrath, joy, sympathy, pity, jealousy, abhorrence and loathing. The warning 'do not grieve the Spirit' is meaningless if God cannot grieve. Denying this brings serious consequences.

Calvary was not just 'another day in the life of God', strictly dispassionate. Was there nothing in the feelings of the Father corresponding to the cry of dereliction in his Son? Can a loving Father crush his innocent Son dispassionately? Does the Father watch apathetically as he sees Jesus writhe and bleed? Does he turn his back in abandonment so effortlessly? Surely Calvary is *the* proof that God is not a stone.

There is another baffling mystery. How can any sane person not love Christ? How can such a great God show such great love to such great sinners deserving such great punishment, yet they refuse? How can God offer rebels such a free and full salvation yet they will not avail themselves? Truly there is mystery in providence.

DISCUSS IT

QUESTIONS FOR DISCUSSION

1. *What do Ecclesiastes 11:5-6 and Luke 13:1-5 tell us about interpreting providence?*

2. *Read Judges 2:18-21; Isaiah 63:9; Jeremiah 15:5; and Joel 2:17. What do they teach regarding emotions in God?*

3. *Read Psalm 73:21-28. Identify the points where it reinforces the message in Job.*

CHAPTER EIGHT

'WHERE CAN WISDOM BE FOUND?'

LOOK IT UP

BIBLE READING

Job 28

INTRODUCTION

'But where can wisdom be found? Where does understanding dwell?' (28:12).

The book of Job belongs to the genre called 'Wisdom Literature' (along with Proverbs and Ecclesiastes). This literature is concerned with *reality* and man's perception of reality. Wisdom is all about understanding *order* in the universe, the meaning of a thing and its connection with other things. That order is hidden behind the visible events of daily life. So wisdom deals with what you cannot see behind what you can see. Wisdom involves knowing the way things 'are', and living sensibly in the light of it.

In the book of Job, the call for 'wisdom' comes in the context of an innocent man suffering terribly. How is this crisis to be explained? What is the *order* or the *reality* behind Job's ordeal? Why *are* things so unpleasant for Job? Where does understanding dwell?

Job's three counsellors presume to have 'wisdom' in this matter. They claim to understand the *order* behind what has happened to Job. But with wearisome and increasingly aggressive speeches, they reduced wisdom to a matter of cause and effect: Job suffers because Job sinned. But they were wrong, and Job knew that true wisdom would yield a different answer. What was it? Better still, where is wisdom in all its fulness? Where is the explanation of all reality, not just Job's reality? Where is the order behind this whole universe?

'Where can wisdom be found? Where does understanding dwell?' That is the question. It is useful to explore three issues here.

1. Why does Job ask it? What has happened in the immediate context to prompt that question?
2. How does Job answer it?
3. How does Job develop the answer?

1. Why does Job ask it?

The conversation had reached an impasse by chapter 24. Job's excellent speech about the 'mystery of providence' (Job 21) has obviously fallen on deaf ears. The response by Eliphaz totally ignored the cogency of Job's point. He kept on arguing 'cause and effect': 'Is it for your piety that he rebukes you and brings charges against you? Is not your wickedness great? Are not your sins endless?' (22:4-5). Worse still, he follows that with an appalling list of false charges against Job:

> 'You demanded security from your brothers for no reason; you stripped men of their clothing, leaving them naked. You gave no water to the weary and you withheld food from the hungry, though you were a powerful man, owning land — an honoured man, living on it. And you sent widows away empty-handed and broke the strength of the fatherless. That is why snares are all around you, why sudden peril terrifies you, why it is so dark you cannot see, and why a flood of water covers you' (22:6-11).

This is obviously false because it is contrary to God's testimony about Job: 'There is no one on earth like him; he is blameless and upright, a man who fears God and shuns evil' (1:8). God repeated it even more emphatically: 'There is no one on earth like him; he is blameless and upright, a man who fears God and shuns evil. And he still maintains his integrity, though you incited me against him to ruin him without any reason' (2:3).

What can Job say? Is there any point in speaking again? Probably not, yet he tries. He returns to the mystery of providence. He explains again the difficulty of understanding God's ways. Man's perception of reality cannot be trusted. It can give a distorted impression of God, as if he turns a blind eye to evil. He does not seem to judge evildoers (24:1). Thieves keep on stealing (24:2-3), the strong keep oppressing the weak (24:4, 10), and their victims struggle to survive the ordeal (24:5-8). But God does not act and he does not seem to care: 'The groans of the dying rise from the city, and the souls of the wounded cry out for help. But God charges no one with wrongdoing' (24:12).

Do not misunderstand Job: he is not impugning God in any way! He is simply showing his friends that they are talking foolishly. They cannot explain everything by cause and effect. The *order* behind the events of life is far more complex than that. Job is about to tell them about wisdom far beyond our limited human resources, the wisdom of God (Job 28), which alone can explain all things. He prepares them for that by exposing the limitations of their wisdom.

Job explores the 'out of sight, out of mind' agenda. A large proportion of crime is committed under cover of darkness. 'There are those who rebel against the light, who do not know its ways or stay in its paths' (24:13). Is that why God seems to take little notice? To be specific: 'When daylight is gone, the murderer rises up and kills the poor and needy; in the night he steals forth like a thief. The eye of the adulterer watches for dusk; he thinks, "No eye will see me," and he keeps his face concealed. In the dark, men break into houses, but by day they shut themselves in; they want nothing to do with the light. For all of them, deep darkness is their morning; they make friends with the terrors of darkness' (24:14-17).

Like Adam hiding behind trees, the criminal deludes himself that God cannot see him. But God does see; so why does it seem like he does not? Why does he not act? Job is defying his friends to explain what God is doing here. Human wisdom is out of its depth.

Of course God is in control! Of course the wicked will be judged! Of course God cares! Of course we can make some general deductions about what might be happening behind the scenes. 'But God drags away the mighty by his power; though they become established, they have no assurance of life. He may let them rest in a feeling of security, but his eyes are on their ways. For a little while they are exalted, and then they are gone; they are brought low and gathered up like all others; they are cut off like ears of corn' (24:22-24).

As general principles, those notions are true. We expect justice to prevail sooner or later. But this is only a very broad theodicy (defence of God's justice). It rightly asserts that justice wins in the end. But it cannot explain why justice is often trampled under foot along the way! And it does not even begin to explain innocent suffering! Even at its best, human wisdom cannot account for life's anomalies. Much greater wisdom is needed. Job ended his speech by throwing down the gauntlet: 'If this is not so, who can prove me false and reduce my words to nothing?'

(v. 25). 'Prove me wrong if you can, but at least do me the courtesy of dealing with my words. Stop ignoring my point!'

Bildad's reply (Job 25) was brief and irrelevant. He made no attempt to take up Job's challenge. He did not contest anything Job had said. He spoke less than forty words, merely rehashing the doctrine of universal sin that Job has never disputed. 'How then can a man be righteous before God? How can one born of woman be pure? If even the moon is not bright and the stars are not pure in his eyes, how much less man, who is but a maggot — a son of man, who is only a worm!' (25:4-6). The crude implication is that Job's suffering is no less than a maggot deserves.

Job is becoming annoyed. His response to this smug arrogance is deservedly sharp and tinged with sarcasm (Job 26 - 27). 'Then Job replied: "How you have helped the powerless! How you have saved the arm that is feeble! What advice you have offered to one without wisdom! And what great insight you have displayed! Who has helped you utter these words? And whose spirit spoke from your mouth?"' (26:1-4). In other words, 'What a brilliant speech, Bildad! That really helps a lot! What profound insights you offer to underlings like me who lack wisdom! Surely this display of genius is super-human! Some higher power has helped you. What spirit was it?'

Job reasserts the infinite wisdom of God (26:5-14). He understands things where men can only guess, such as death and destruction (26:5-6) and how the cosmos holds together (26:7-13). 'He wraps up the waters in his clouds, yet the clouds do not burst under their weight' (26:8).

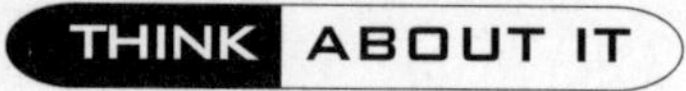

THINK ABOUT IT

What a sobering point!

Job described God's wisdom in the clouds, the horizon, the sun and moon and the oceans as merely 'the outer fringe of his works' and 'the faint whisper we hear of him!' (26:14). Man is right out of this league! 'Who then can understand the thunder of his power?' Complete mysteries for men are kindergarten issues for God. If we cannot fathom these 'outer fringes' or 'faint whispers' of God's wisdom, how incompetent we are with the greater things, his 'thunder'! Humility depends on us recognizing this truth.

Then Job immediately reasserted his innocence. His suffering is not a matter of justice. It is not due to cause and effect. It is not deserved.

> 'Job continued his discourse: "As surely as God lives, who has denied me justice, the Almighty, who has made me taste bitterness of soul, as long as I have life within me, the breath of God in my nostrils, my

> lips will not speak wickedness, and my tongue will utter no deceit. I will never admit you are in the right; till I die, I will not deny my integrity. I will maintain my righteousness and never let go of it; my conscience will not reproach me as long as I live"' (27:1-6).

His righteous indignation included an imprecatory cry: 'May my enemies be like the wicked, my adversaries like the unjust!' (27:7). Finally he vents his frustration at his counsellors: 'You have all seen this yourselves. Why then this meaningless talk?' (27:12). Why do you keep on making statements of the obvious? Why keep on with your irrelevant arguments? Job is weary of listening to pseudo-wisdom, and so is the reader. That is the context for his wisdom poem (Job 28). That is why Job asked the fundamental question, 'Where can wisdom be found? Where does understanding dwell?'

2. How does Job answer it?

It is helpful to go straight to the answer before returning to see how Job develops it. His first answer is negative. Wisdom does not come from the finite creation. 'Where can wisdom be found? Where does understanding dwell? Man does not comprehend its worth; it cannot be found in the land of the living' (28:12-13).

It is not found in the deepest place or for sale in any market place. 'The deep says, "It is not in me"; the sea says, "It is not with me." It cannot be bought with the finest gold, nor can its price be weighed in silver' (28:14-15). Even if wisdom was for sale, you could not afford it: 'Neither gold nor crystal can compare with it, nor can it be had for jewels of gold. Coral and jasper are not worthy of mention; the price of wisdom is beyond rubies. The topaz of Cush cannot compare with it; it cannot be bought with pure gold' (28:17-19).

So Job repeats the question: 'Where then does wisdom come from? Where does understanding dwell?' (28:20). And he repeats his previous answer. Wisdom is not found in the mundane creaturely realm: 'It is hidden from the eyes of every living thing, concealed even from the birds of the air' (28:21). Beyond the shadows of this life, in the depths of the nether world, there is only a rumour that wisdom even exists: 'Destruction and Death say, "Only a rumour of it has reached our ears"' (28:22).

Finally, the truth about wisdom is announced: 'God understands the way to it and he alone knows where it dwells, for he views the ends of the earth and sees everything under the heavens. When he established the force of the wind and measured out the waters, when he made a decree for the rain and a path for the thunderstorm, then he looked at wisdom and appraised it; he confirmed it and tested it. And he said to man, "The fear of the Lord — that is wisdom, and to shun evil is understanding"' (28:23-28). In other words, perfect wisdom is a divine attribute. We rightly sing:

Immortal, invisible, God only wise,
In light inaccessible hid from our eyes.[1]

Christian worship says: 'to the only wise God be glory for ever through Jesus Christ' (Romans 16:27).

Job alerts us to several aspects of wisdom. As a divine property, it corresponds with other divine attributes, especially *omniscience*. Wisdom requires knowledge. Only the all-knowing God can be all wise: 'God ... alone knows where it dwells, for he views the ends of the earth and sees everything under the heavens' (28:23-24).

Wisdom is also related to omnipotence. Infinite wisdom guided infinite power in creating the cosmos out of nothing. Wisdom designed it all. By wisdom it holds together. Each part and each moment serves the whole. Creation is a tangible expression of God's pre-existing wisdom: 'When he established the force of the wind and measured out the waters, when he made a decree for the rain and a path for the thunderstorm, then he looked at wisdom and appraised it; he confirmed it and tested it' (28:25-27). So the height of folly is to deny God because that denies wisdom. 'The fool says in his heart, "There is no God"' (Psalm 14:1). The theory of macroevolution is a common form of that folly. To suggest that the universe originated randomly, without wisdom causing it, is madness.

But if wisdom belongs to God, can man be truly wise? Yes, and Job explains how. Wisdom at the human level lies in having a proper relationship with God. 'The fear of the Lord — that is wisdom, and to shun evil is understanding.'

REMEMBER THIS

So Job is wise!

See the connection in the text! At the start of the book God said that, more than all men on earth, Job 'fears God and shuns evil' (1:8). Since wisdom is now defined with those exact words ('fearing the Lord and shunning evil') God has declared Job the wisest man around. Job understands the order of the cosmos better than his counsellors. Job understands reality. The gaps in his knowledge do not make him less wise. Rather, he trusts God whose knowledge has no gaps. That is wisdom.

Wisdom is a spiritual issue, a religious issue. Wisdom is a reverent fear of God. Wisdom is a life governed by his commands. Unbelief is the opposite of wisdom: so is all manner of evil. Job's conclusion about wisdom is identical to that in the other 'Wisdom' books. The preacher finishes his wisdom literature saying, 'Now all has been heard; here is the conclusion of the matter: Fear God and keep his commandments, for this is the whole duty of man' (Ecclesiastes 12:13). The book of Proverbs resonates with statements like: 'The fear of the LORD is the beginning of wisdom, and knowledge of the Holy One is understanding' (Proverbs 9:10).

3. How does Job develop the answer?

Job uses the *a-fortiori* method of answering (arguing from strong to stronger). He shows how great human wisdom is in order to show how much greater God's wisdom is. As God's image bearer, man is the supreme creature with skills and abilities far beyond all others. Man has plumbed mysteries unknown to other creatures. He has searched out unseen treasures and gone into places no other creature could go.

He mines silver and gold (28:1). He understands how to shine light into the deepest recesses: 'Man puts an end to the darkness; he searches the farthest recesses for ore in the blackest darkness' (28:3-4). Man not only harvests food from earth's surface, he also harvests its gems from deep underground. 'The earth, from which food comes, is transformed below as by fire; sapphires come from its rocks, and its dust contains nuggets of gold' (vv. 5-6). The other creatures pale into insignificance: 'No bird of prey knows that hidden path, no falcon's eye has seen it. Proud beasts do not set foot on it, and no lion prowls there' (vv. 7-8).

Man can overturn mountains in his mining exploits: 'Man's hand assaults the flinty rock and lays bare the roots of the mountains' (v. 9). He discriminates between valuable gems and worthless dust: 'He tunnels through the rock; his eyes see all its treasures' (v. 10). He takes advantage of the streams in sifting out precious stones (v. 11). There is no doubt that man has been exceedingly gifted by his Creator. But for all of that, man is very limited. He is faced with mysteries all around. Where can wisdom be found? Where does understanding dwell? 'God understands the way to it and he alone knows where it dwells' (v. 23). Compared to God, man is abysmally ignorant! Man's rejection of God is the folly that destroys him. Man's fear of God is the wisdom that saves him for ever.

QUESTIONS FOR DISCUSSION

DISCUSS IT

1. *Proverbs 8 is a famous description of wisdom. How many similarities does it have with Job 28?*

2. *From the following texts, what has Jesus Christ got to do with wisdom? (Matthew 7:24-27; 1 Corinthians 1:22-24, 30; Ephesians 1:7-10; Colossians 2:2-3).*

3. *What is the connection between Scripture and wisdom? (Read 2 Timothy 3:12-17; Psalm 19:7-14; Psalm 119:97-105).*

CHAPTER NINE

GOSPEL CONCEPTS IN JOB

LOOK IT UP

BIBLE READING

Job 9:32-35; 19:25-27; 38 - 41

INTRODUCTION

We have already seen some important gospel themes in the book of Job. Lines are drawn in Job leading inevitably to Christ. Jesus is the ultimate Job, the ultimate righteous man suffering to ruin the intentions of Satan. In particular, three gospel concepts stand out in Job:

1. The mediator concept (9:32-35)
2. The resurrection concept (19:25-27)
3. The revelation concept (38 - 41)

1. The mediator concept

The need for a mediator became clear to Job as his sufferings progressed. He had been thinking about the vast disparity between God and man. God is so great. 'His wisdom is profound, his power is vast' (9:4), he 'moves mountains' (9:5), and he 'shakes the earth' (v. 6). He not only 'speaks to the sun and it does not shine' (v. 7), but 'He performs wonders that cannot be fathomed' (v. 10). By contrast, man is tiny. Even our questions are out of order. 'Who can say to him, "What are you doing?"' (v. 12). Man is incompetent before the Almighty: 'How then can I dispute with him?' (v. 14). 'If it is a matter of strength, he is mighty! And if it is a matter of justice, who will summon him?' (v. 19). 'Though one wished to dispute with him, he could not answer him one time out of a thousand' (v. 3).

Job reels at the enormity of it: 'I cannot deal with God face to face. I'm only a man. Even if I were perfect I could hardly have a little fireside chat with God.' 'Though I were innocent, I could not answer him; I could only plead with my Judge for mercy' (v. 15). Before God I'm helpless. I couldn't even begin to ask questions. As soon as I saw him I would need to ask for mercy. The difference between God and man is infinite! So Job concluded: 'He is not a man like me that I might answer him, that we might confront each other in court. If only there were someone to arbitrate between us, to lay his hand upon us both, someone to remove God's rod from me, so that his terror would frighten me no more. Then I would speak up without fear of him, but as it now stands with me, I cannot' (vv. 32-35).

Job saw the need for a 'mediator' (NKJV) between God and man, an 'arbitrator' (NIV), an 'umpire' (NASB). Someone is needed to solve this problem of two very unequal parties, someone who can bridge the enormous gap between God and man. Someone with a foot in both camps is needed; someone perfectly at ease with God and with man. Is there someone who can represent the interests of God and man without compromise, who can lay his hand on both? Job wants someone who can bring 'him up to God's level and God down to Job's level', someone who can take away God's rod from him and who can cast out terror and enable him to speak before God without dread. So he yearns for a mediator, to reconcile God and man, bringing the two together. He will need all the capacities of God (to cope with the Almighty), and the incapacities of man (to identify with Job).

Job was longing for exactly what God wanted him to long for, and what every thinking man should long for. He longed for exactly what God had planned to provide from all eternity. We are privileged to know the ultimate answer to Job's prayer: 'For there is one God and one mediator between God and men, the man Christ Jesus' (1 Timothy 2:5). Of course Job did not know that. He was not aware of the incarnation of the second person in the Trinity. Job could not know about Jesus of Nazareth being fully God and fully man. But he recognized the need. It is a key gospel concept in Job. In chapter 9 we shall see how Elihu is the immediate answer to Job's prayer. He plays the role of mediator for Job, providing a further development of this gospel paradigm.

2. The resurrection concept

'I know that my Redeemer lives, and that in the end he will stand upon the earth. And after my skin has been destroyed, yet in my flesh I will see God; I myself will see him with my own eyes — I, and not another. How my heart yearns within me!' (19:25-27).

Though the Hebrew text is difficult, some conclusions are warranted. Job is sure that God saves his believing people from death, in death, through death, and despite death. That is what 'redeemer' seems to mean in this context. Even if his present sufferings stop, Job knows that he will die one day, but that will not be the end of him. He believes in life beyond the grave, and not only life, but life with God: 'and after my skin has been destroyed, yet in my flesh I will see God'. The death of the body is not the end of the body. The skin (body/flesh) will be destroyed but it will live again and 'see God'. To emphasize this bodily resurrection, Job adds: 'I myself will see him with my own eyes — I, and not another' (19:27).

So he is not talking about the 'intermediate state' prior to the resurrection on Judgement Day. He is not talking about the souls of God's people going immediately into the presence of God while their bodies lie in the grave as dust returns to dust. No, he is talking about something later on, when the dust is reconstituted into a living body. He refers to the dust being revived, raised up and resurrected as the body it once was, only far more glorious and capable. He is talking about 'I myself

... I, and not another.' The same body that died is to be raised up. This is not a mere peripheral or minor aspect of Job's beliefs. It is vital and central to his faith, and he longed for it: 'How my heart yearns within me!'

The idea of resurrection does not begin in the New Testament. Here we see it in perhaps the oldest book in the Bible. Remember also Abraham's resurrection faith. He believed that God was able to resurrect Isaac (Hebrews 11:19). According to the New Testament, the resurrection is the crucial doctrine. Everything hangs on it! If the dead are not raised then not even Christ is raised. That would mean faith is vain and Christians should be pitied more than all men (1 Corinthians 15). Paul looks forward to the resurrection as the climax of all history, 'the redemption of our bodies' (Romans 8:23). The earth will be set free from the curse of sin to enjoy the glorious liberty of the sons of God. Peter said it is the basis and foundation of our hope: we are 'given ... new birth into a living hope through the resurrection of Jesus Christ from the dead' (1 Peter 1:3).

On that great day when Christ returns our mortal bodies shall lose all mortality, all corruption, and all corruptibility. There will be no more sickness or suffering, no more tears, no more 'skin destroyed'. Death is swallowed up in victory. Victory has the last say, not death! And Job knew it (though not with the same clarity that came with later revelation). The Beatitude announces: 'Blessed are the pure in heart, for they will see God' (Matthew 5:8).

It is worth noting that chapter 19 sheds more light on Job's famous earlier words: 'Though he slay me, yet will I hope in him' (13:15). It could also be translated as 'Though he slay me, yet will I serve him'. Normally we take it to mean that Job will keep on loving God right up to the point of death, implying that then he can love or serve him no more. Thus he means, 'Only death can stop me serving God.' But, informed by chapter 19, it means far more. Job is really saying, 'Even if he slays me I'll still be loving him. Death will not stop my service of God or my hope. I will serve God beyond death!' Job is convinced about a true resurrection to life and fellowship with God after death.

3. The revelation concept

Job is a desperate man. He is seeking help and guidance. He urgently needs a sure word of truth to cling to. He has heard vast amounts of guidance, all unsatisfactory. Even his wise meditations gave no relief. Finally help arrived, coming from the mouth of God. During the whole long ordeal God had not spoken to Job. But at last God broke his silence by speaking out of the whirlwind (chapters 38 - 41). And at last Job had sufficient guidance. At last Job was content though, curiously,

God did not say everything Job may have wished for. In particular, he deliberately avoided the one thing Job was keen to know: why he was suffering. However, what he *did* tell Job was quite sufficient! This principle lies at the heart of true godliness in every age.

Orthodox Christianity believes in the sufficiency of Scripture. The sixty-six books of the Bible constitute God's full revelation in this age. The Bible does not tell us all we want to know, but it tells us all we need. God's will is either explicit (written down in the Bible) or implicit (the good and logical deductions from Scripture).

THINK ABOUT IT

Why do some people disagree?

Jesus said, 'When he, the Spirit of truth, comes, he will guide you into all truth. He will not speak on his own; he will speak only what he hears; and he will tell you what is yet to come' (John 16:13). This is commonly misunderstood to support ongoing revelations today. In fact it refers to the inspiration of the New Testament writings, finished around A.D. 90 in the book of Revelation. This work of the Holy Spirit cannot be pushed beyond the Apostolic age. We are not still in the process of being 'guided into all the truth'. How do we know?

We know by observing proper interpretive principles! Jesus made that promise to a specific audience, his small band of Jewish disciples living around A.D. 30. It was to that precise group that Jesus made the promise. *They* were about to be cast out of the synagogues and killed (v. 2). *They* were in no fit state to hear the extra truths that Jesus wished to tell them because they were so distressed (vv. 6 & 12). *They* would receive the full disclosures of the Holy Spirit. *They* would be told all that Christ wanted the church to know. To *them* would come 'all the truth'. Jesus made the promise to them in Israel in the first half of the first century, not to us in the first years of the twenty-first century.

The question is, 'Did Jesus keep his promise?' Did the church, prior to the death of the last Apostle (John), come to possess 'all the truth'? Did the Holy Spirit 'deliver the goods' as promised? Of course, and it is preserved in the full sixty-six-book canon of Scripture. If anyone says that the church is still being led into 'all the truth' they are burdened with the conclusion that Jesus did not keep his word then, and at no stage does the church have 'all the truth'. Even 2,000 years later we are still receiving updates, and even they are lost for ever, 'blowing in the wind'. The whole notion is untenable and dangerous.

Job's sufferings were not overcome by any other message or vision, although we need to remember that one of his friends actually tried that (4:12-19). Eliphaz claimed that God had spoken to him in a dream. He claimed it was a very real and deep spiritual experience that made his bones shake and his hair stand up. Eliphaz said he heard a hushed voice giving him a message for Job, and that he saw something: 'a spirit glided past my face … but I could not tell what it was' (4:15-16). As we saw in chapter 5, this guidance by experience is dangerous. Guidance from feelings and hunches is mere subjective mysticism. The book of Job exposes it as nonsense. God certainly did not give such a message to Eliphaz. God did not agree with it.

Job learned not to go beyond God's word revelation. Job's friends also learned the same. It is a serious error to suggest that Scripture is not a full and sufficient revelation from God. The strength of the Protestant Reformation was its insistence on *Sola Scriptura* (Scripture alone). True Christianity has always rejected 'messages from God' beyond the sixty-six books of Scripture. To submit in conscience to 'extra-biblical' messages is essentially cultic and sectarian. Whether they be visions of saints, or Mary, or Christ; whether they are the opinions and dogmas of tradition, or the writings of cult leaders, or the self-deluded claims of modern men boasting 'a word from the Lord', they have no place in our theological system. 'The whole counsel of God concerning all things necessary for his own glory, man's salvation, faith and life is either expressly set down in Scripture, or by good and necessary consequence may be deduced from Scripture: into which nothing at any time is to be added whether by new revelations of the Spirit or traditions of men' (*Westminster Confession of Faith*, 1:6).

These gospel concepts in Job are vital for all of us: the mediator, the resurrection, and God's revelation. Ultimately you must abandon yourself to Christ. He is the mediator. You cannot face God without him. He is the resurrection. You cannot avoid the second death without him. The Bible is God's written word about Jesus the incarnate 'word'. May you be his and he yours for ever!

QUESTIONS FOR DISCUSSION

1. *What do we learn about the Mediator in John 14:6-11?*

2. *What encouragements derive from having Jesus as our Mediator? (See Hebrews 2:11-18 and 4:14-16.)*

3. *Is it right to conclude from 1 Corinthians 15 that 'Whoever denies the resurrection denies Christianity'?*

4. *From both the explicit statements and logical implications of Romans 13:1-8, what is 'the will of God' for citizens and civil governments?*

CHAPTER TEN

WHO IS ELIHU?

LOOK IT UP

BIBLE READING

Job 32 - 37

INTRODUCTION

The interpretation of the Elihu narratives is a classic Old Testament problem area. The final human actor in the drama of the book, Elihu makes four speeches occupying six chapters. Younger than Job and his three counsellors, Elihu has obviously heard what they have said to each other since he interacts with it. He acts as a strictly impartial third party, taking issue with Job on some matters and with the counsellors on other matters. His ultimate aim is 'to justify' Job (33:32, NASB), to clear Job, to bring good news to him. In doing so, Elihu makes incredible claims about himself (see below). As a result it is common for commentators to say some very harsh things about him. Here is a typical sample:

> 'Elihu is mad at the world ... a brash young man ... an angry young man ... typical of the young he is angry, impatient, and arrogant'.[1] And a similar view: 'Like many young Theologians, Elihu had a bit of youthful conceit in his speeches.'[2] One

writer entitles the whole Elihu narrative as 'The Angry Young Man'.[3]

This seems to be a common view. Elihu is seen as full of words and full of himself, adding nothing new to the debate, merely rehashing what Job or the counsellors have said. The Elihu speeches are regarded as the 'low part' of the book. The more liberal theologians dismiss the whole section as being non-canonical. Yet remarkably, neither Job nor God take exception to anything Elihu says! Job answers everyone else, but not a word against Elihu. God rebukes everyone else (including Job) but again, not a word against Elihu. A more careful look at the text and context will provide a better understanding of who Elihu is.

This issue demonstrates an important principle.

The Elihu narrative illustrates how the Old Testament Scriptures need to be understood in the light of the New Testament writings. The veiled shadows and enigmas of the thirty-nine Old Testament books are to be seen in the clearer light of the twenty-seven New Testament books. It is the duty of every interpreter to look for the theological and covenantal connections. The gospel is the interpretive grid for every Old Testament text. It is the neglect of this that has caused Elihu's defamation.

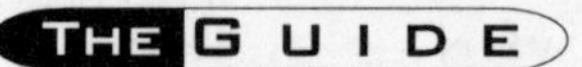

There are four lines of evidence that need to be appreciated:

1. Elihu's credentials,
2. His claims,
3. His context,
4. His message.

Having done that, we can consider how Job understood his message.

1. Elihu's credentials

The writer provides us with a very detailed 'birth certificate' for Elihu.

a. His name: (אֱלִיהוּא) means 'My God is he', or 'My God is', or 'My God is God'. In effect, Elihu is a Hebrew word that brings up all the same connotations as 'Yahweh' (I am, God is, the God who is God).

b. His Father's name: Barachel (בָּרַכְאֵל) means 'God blesses', or 'The God who blesses', or 'God has blessed'.

c. His clan: He is descended from **Buz**, which is Abraham's family tree (see Genesis 22:21). Elihu belongs to the ancient covenant line. He is 'seed of Abraham'.

d. His family: He is from the family of **Ram** (meaning lofty or exalted). There is an important genealogy in Ruth 4:18-22. Ram is the forefather of David. Elihu is in the line of David, of the tribe of Judah, the Messianic line.

So here is a man whose name is equivalent to God's name, a man who is the son of 'the God who blesses', who is the seed of Abraham, and who is in the Davidic (Messianic) line of Judah. When the book of Job was written, these facts would not have seemed important. Their compound significance only becomes apparent to those who have a New Testament. But since we have the wider picture, how can we fail to see the significance? Do we write this off as mere 'coincidence'? Is this mere incidental detail? No, the pedigree of Elihu screams out gospel connections. Do we know anyone in the New Testament fitting this agenda? If so, we have to be very careful in our handling of the Elihu narratives.

2. His claims

Elihu makes massive claims about himself. They are so extraordinary and so egocentric that, if they are untrue (as so many interpreters say), then we have no choice but to take a very negative view of Elihu, denouncing him as an arrogant upstart. But if these claims are true (as I suggest they are) then our conclusion will be entirely different. He claims:

a. Supernatural wisdom. He says he is wise by 'the breath of the Almighty'. He has a wisdom not common to man, well beyond his age. He claims to be inspired. His words have the status of God's words. 'So Elihu ... said: "I am young in years, and you are old; that is why I was fearful, not daring to tell you what I know. I thought, 'Age should speak; advanced years should teach wisdom.' But it is the spirit in a man, the breath of the Almighty, that gives him understanding. It is not only the old who are wise, not only the aged who understand what is right"' (32:6-9).

b. Complete honesty. He has no partiality and uses no flattery: 'I will show partiality to no one, nor will I flatter any man; for if I were skilled in flattery, my Maker would soon take me away' (32:21-22).

c. Uprightness and sincerity. 'My words come from an upright heart; my lips sincerely speak what I know. The Spirit of God has made me; the breath of the Almighty gives me life' (33:3-4). His words 'The Spirit of God has made me; the breath of the Almighty gives me life' seem to mean more than what is common to all men. Otherwise why bother saying it? It seems to mean that in his counsel to Job, Elihu claims the integrity of the Holy Spirit. This is borne out by another claim.

d. Perfect knowledge. 'Elihu continued: "Bear with me a little longer and I will show you that there is more to be said on God's behalf. I get my knowledge from afar; I will ascribe justice to my Maker. Be assured that my words are not false; one perfect in knowledge is with you"' (36:1-4). This is a very big claim!

e. *Unrebuttable, final wisdom.* 'Therefore I say: "Listen to me; I too will tell you what I know. I waited while you spoke, I listened to your reasoning; while you were searching for words, I gave you my full attention. But not one of you has proved Job wrong; none of you has answered his arguments"' (32:10-12). 'Answer me then, if you can; prepare yourself and confront me' (33:5). 'Hear my words, you wise men; listen to me, you men of learning' (34:2). 'If you have understanding, hear this; listen to what I say' (34:16).

These are astonishing assertions. He not only claims to be unanswerable (throwing out the challenge for Job to try if he can), but he also regards his words as the essence of wisdom to which all 'wise men' must listen.

f. *New light on the Job mystery.* Elihu denies that he is rehashing old views. The old opinions were vain. They failed. But he claims to have new light. He is bursting to reveal it like new wine bursting wineskins.

> 'I waited while you spoke, I listened to your reasoning; while you were searching for words, I gave you my full attention. But not one of you

has proved Job wrong; none of you has answered his arguments. Do not say, "We have found wisdom; let God refute him, not man." But Job has not marshalled his words against me, and I will not answer him with your arguments. They are dismayed and have no more to say; words have failed them. Must I wait, now that they are silent, now that they stand there with no reply? I too will have my say; I too will tell what I know. For I am full of words, and the spirit within me compels me; inside I am like bottled-up wine, like new wineskins ready to burst. I must speak and find relief; I must open my lips and reply. I will show partiality to no one, nor will I flatter any man; for if I were skilled in flattery, my Maker would soon take me away. But now, Job, listen to my words; pay attention to everything I say' (32:11 – 33:1).

Does all this remind you of anyone else who made the same egocentric claims? A man whom the 'scholars' and 'intellectuals' of his day also dismissed as an arrogant, blasphemous upstart? The fact is that Jesus of Nazareth made all these claims! Isn't he the man of complete honesty, 'full of truth'? Isn't he the ultimate man of the Spirit, upright and sincere? Isn't he the one who is perfect in knowledge, Immanuel, God with us? Isn't he the one to whom all wise men must listen otherwise they are like fools building houses with no foundations? Isn't he the one who brings light to shine in darkness, bringing ultimate purpose to innocent suffering? If we dismiss Elihu for making these claims are we not wiping out an Old Testament pointer to Jesus? Are we not in danger of erasing the gospel pattern in Job?

It is especially important that we understand Elihu's gospel message (33:23-30). He lifts the explanation for what has happened to Job to a new and higher plane. He deals with the mystery of why God's most righteous man (1:1, 8) is suffering so horribly. His explanation is full of gospel emblems. He shows that somehow God uses the sufferings of an innocent man to bring about the richest blessings possible for sinners, 'a mediator, one out of a thousand, to tell a man what is right for him ... to spare him from going down to the pit'. It leads man to find acceptance with God (33:26), saying, 'He redeemed my soul from going down to the pit, and I shall live to enjoy the light' (33:28). While the Hebrew is not easy, and the answer is still incomplete and sketchy (cast in the enigmatic language of Jewish Wisdom Literature), we should have no doubt that Job grasped the essential points of Elihu's message.

In summary we may paraphrase Elihu's revelation this way: 'Somehow, innocent suffering is connected with being ransomed from sin. Somehow, the greatest blessing for sinful man is connected with the greatest suffering of an innocent man. Somehow, the way God will show the favour of his face is by withdrawing the favour of his face. Somehow, the permission of God to let Satan afflict his choicest servant will redeem Satan's servants from the pit.'

Job had no need to answer because it thrilled his soul and reaffirmed more clearly his own famous speech, 'I know that my Redeemer lives' (19:25). Elihu made sense when no one else did. Now Job is composed and settled despite his trials. At last he has an answer that harmonizes with everything he knows and believes, everything he has been answering back to the three counsellors. They told Job that the whole issue was about *bad news* (Job's secret sin which he refused to own up to), and that it was wicked to talk about God willing an innocent man such gross sufferings. But Elihu told Job that the whole issue was about *good news,* that God was indicating (through Job) a gracious plan to redeem sinners by the sufferings of a good man. The two sets of answers are poles apart.

3. His context

Who is Elihu? The picture building up already suggests that he is an Old Testament picture of the mediator Jesus Christ.

There are two further observations regarding the structure of the book in support of that view.

1. The mediator Job was looking for

Elihu is the answer to Job's prayer in chapter 9. There he admitted his incapacity before God. God is too great for man to talk with on level terms. Compare Job in 9:32-35 and Elihu in 33:5-7. Job said God is too big to confront. Elihu said, 'Prepare yourself and confront me.' Job desires a mediator, a man like himself who can 'lay his hand upon us both' (represent God and man). Elihu says, 'I am just like you before God; I too have been taken from clay.' Job prayed for someone sent from God that he could talk to, who would not alarm or frighten him. Elihu said, 'No fear of me should alarm you, nor should my hand be heavy upon you.' If we believe in the integrity of the author and the logic of his book then *he* tells us who Elihu is. He is the mediator sent by God, a man of like nature with Job, who speaks for both God and man, the answer to Job's prayers and needs.

2. His location within the book

Elihu fits exactly where a thoughtful writer would put a mediator: between God and man. Notice that the section concerning Elihu fits in between two very significant markers in the book. The first marker is 31:40: 'The words of Job are ended.' Men have had their say. The problem remains. The second marker is 38:1: 'Then the LORD answered Job out of the storm.' God is about to speak. He has remained silent on earth during the whole process thus far. In between these two large sections we have the Elihu narratives. All six chapters in between are literally *mediatory*: someone speaking between man and God. In the last verse before Elihu speaks, mere men cease speaking. In the verse after Elihu speaks, God speaks. God's speech inherently endorses all that Elihu has said. What a brilliant composition the book of Job is, right down to its structure!

Who is Elihu? He is an Old Testament picture of the mediator, Jesus Christ. His message is core gospel. His words are agreeable to both God and Job. Whether or not you call it true typology (as I am inclined to do), the fact is that Elihu cannot be dismissed as 'an arrogant young upstart' without doing considerable damage to the integrity of the book of Job or the nature of Scripture, or both.

4. His message

What message did Job understand from Elihu? What comfort did he derive? What is the crucial point he would have reflected on after that encounter? His understanding would not be the same as ours now, with all our advantage of hindsight. We have the whole picture before us, the beginning and the end of redemptive history explained in the sixty-six books. We can see the typology and the repeated paradigms. But it was different for Job. He lived in the 'small picture'. He was moving in the very indistinct shadows of early redemptive history, shadows which were drawn long since the light was just dawning. In Job's situation, what could you have gleaned from Elihu? From the words he explicitly spoke, and from their 'good and necessary consequences', what was the message of Elihu? In essence, the answer is:

> 'Job, I have been sent by God to give you the final word and the right interpretation of your sufferings. It is not on account of faults in you. Your three counsellors are all wrong in denying innocent suffering. There are spiritual issues here that God has not revealed to you, but you are vindicated. Though pushed to the limit, your faith has prevailed. You remained loyal to God though it has cost you dearly. God has used your experience to create a paradigm. That paradigm involves innocent suffering and ransom from sin. God connects them somehow so that redemption is achieved, and men are delivered from going down to the pit. God has not yet explained the connection between these things. But you have acted out a redemptive drama that will ultimately be fulfilled and explained in God's choicest servant.'

I think we would be unwise to say more than that. Even in saying that, it is clearer to us than to Job. We are not entitled to read knowledge gleaned from the

New Testament back into the minds of Old Testament characters. We dare not read Job's mind as if he had a copy of the *Westminster Confession of Faith*. What Job gleaned from Elihu was essentially the gospel in its rudimentary form. It satisfied him and gave him composure. The restoration of Job to even greater status than he had at first completes the paradigm of Christ's humiliation and exaltation.

Thus the typology of Christ in the book of Job has two focal points. In Job, Christ is set forth as the innocent sufferer who shoulders the government of God against the assaults of Satan. In Elihu, Christ is set forth as the mediator bringing the final word and interpretation into the human drama.[4]

DISCUSS IT

QUESTIONS FOR DISCUSSION

1. *Consider John 6:35; 8:58; 11:25; 17:1-3; and Matthew 7:24-27. In that light, assess the following: 'These claims of Jesus mean he is either mad, bad, or God.'*

2. *What principles for Old Testament interpretation does Jesus demonstrate in his wilderness temptations? (Read Matthew 4:1-11.)*

3. *If an atheist converts to strict Judaism should Christians rejoice? (See Hebrews 8:6-13.)*

CHAPTER ELEVEN

GOD IN THE STORM

LOOK IT UP

BIBLE READING

Job 38 - 41

INTRODUCTION

Here is the climax of the book of Job. All the minor characters have appeared on stage and played their parts, but now there is an air of expectancy. The theatre is filled with the sound of a rushing wind. Dark clouds are gathering. The atmosphere is electric and highly charged. A storm is brewing. Great drama is about to unfold. The chief character is about to appear: Almighty God comes near. Something big is happening.

What did happen? All Job's questions dissolved. They seemed insignificant, even irrelevant. He met God in the storm: questions do not matter anymore. Yesterday Job had much to ask God. As the list of questions grew, so did his desire for God's answers. He said, 'Let me speak, and you reply' (13:22) and 'Let the Almighty answer me' (31:35). But the appearance of God caused the disappearance of the questions. In Job's own words, 'Surely I spoke of things I did not understand…You said, "Listen now, and I will speak"… My ears had heard of you but now my eyes have seen you. Therefore I despise myself and repent in dust and ashes' (42:3-6).

When we come to *know about* God, lots of questions arise, naturally and logically. But when we come to *know God* even the profound questions become trivial. Of course it is important to know about God. We must have correct views and beliefs about God, but not as an end in itself. That is still only knowing God 'at a distance'. The important thing is to actually know God himself. When that is a reality we are in wonder and awe at his majestic greatness. We are overwhelmed by his intimidating purity, goodness, wisdom, power and self-sufficiency. In our smallness we are so amazed at his enormity that all our questions of 'How this?' and 'Why that?' seem puerile and embarrassing. Job saw that! And that is why he wrote this book. He wants us to see what he saw; to know God in all his glory. The right response to God is not merely belief in him. We are to be enthralled by him, engrossed and dumb-founded by his inexpressible greatness. We should be totally exhilarated in love and wonder, praise, trust, worship and adoration. We must abandon ourselves to the 'immortal, invisible, God only wise'. That was Job's experience in these four chapters. It helps to consider:

1. A proper view of the storm
2. A proper view of God

1. A proper view of the storm

In order to understand this 'storm' (tempest, whirlwind, mighty wind) we need to observe both the immediate and the wider biblical context.

1. The immediate context

God speaks out of '*the* storm' not just *a* storm. The word is quite pointed and definite (הַסְּעָרָה) as if the storm is something already described and anticipated. It forces us to ask: 'Which storm?' There is a clear connection with the previous section (the Elihu speeches). Elihu's last speech announces a coming storm. There is an eerie foreboding. You cannot read chapter 37 without sensing a storm is imminent. The air is restless, the wind is strengthening, and flashes of lightening appear on the horizon. Even in chapter 36 Elihu begins the 'storm' alert:

- God 'fills his hands with lightning' (v. 32)
- 'His thunder announces the coming storm; even the cattle make known its approach' (v. 33)

Elihu senses something dramatic is about to occur: 'At this my heart pounds and leaps from its place' (37:1). 'He unleashes his lightning beneath the whole heaven and sends it to the ends of the earth' (37:3). 'The animals take cover; they remain in their dens. The tempest comes out from its chamber, the cold from the driving winds. The breath of God produces ice, and the broad waters become frozen. He loads the clouds with moisture; he scatters his lightning through them' (37:8-11).

Elihu says that God's voice speaks in the storm (37:1-5). Some people think Elihu is speaking generally, saying all storms, any storms, reveal God. But it is more likely his words contain a prophetic element because he goes on to warn Job (37:14-18), as if God is about to thunder from a storm, as if God is going to appear in person to Job, as if a theophany is expected. The topic is not simply the general revelation of God in 'storms', but a personal appearance of God to Job, his righteous servant. You can feel the urgency: 'Out of the north he comes in golden splendour; God comes in awesome majesty' (37:22). Elihu warned Job not to be foolish by daring to speak or raise questions when it happens, when God Almighty does appear in these cosmic disturbances: 'Tell us what we should say to him... Should he be told that I want to speak? Would any man ask to be swallowed up?' (37:19-20).

How outrageous to raise a mundane human voice in such an electric atmosphere! When a rushing mighty wind announces the appearance of God, will mere flesh and blood declare: 'Listen to me on this momentous occasion'? How preposterous, Job! How outrageous! How audacious! Why do you invite death? The point is also made in 37:21: 'No one can look at the sun, bright as it is in the skies.' How much more impossible it is to look at the one whose glory far outshines the sun.

So Elihu coaches Job in readiness. Then suddenly the storm arrives and God speaks! The storm brewing in chapter 37 is the storm that breaks out in chapter 38.

2. The wider context

It is not unusual for the Bible to link the appearing of God with a storm, a tempest, a mighty wind, or some other cosmic disturbance. This motif suggests that 'the storm' means the storm where God appears. If we notice that larger context, it makes good sense. Thus, the event in Job 38 is not just God speaking, it is God *appearing*; it is a theophany. That is exactly how Job understood it: 'But now my eyes have seen you' (42:5).

The narrative does not begin with the usual formula introducing divine speech ('Now the word of the Lord came to Job, saying'). Rather, the Lord himself came to Job! The whole text (Job 38 - 41) reads exactly like all the other chapters, a personal dialogue with Job. It reads like an actual encounter, an interrogation, just like those between Job and his three friends. Some other theophanies in this bigger picture include:

The Law at Sinai: The mountain was struck with thunder, lightning and thick cloud. Everything shook, because Jehovah had come down personally (Exodus 19).

The day of Pentecost: God came; it was a divine advent, a theophany. There was fire and the whole room filled with the sound of 'a rushing mighty wind' (Acts 2:2, AV).

The prophet's experience: There was a 'windstorm coming out of the North — an immense cloud with flashing lightning and surrounded by brilliant light'. God appears! (Ezekiel 1:4).

Again and again when God appears to men there is some cosmic disturbance. It may be a tempest, or a burning bush (Moses), or darkness at midday with earthquakes and graves opening (Golgotha). For Nahum (1:3), Zechariah (9:14) and Elijah (1 Kings 19:8-12), it is the 'storm' motif again. Not surprisingly, the final great advent of Christ is also set within this theme of cosmic convulsions: 'Immediately after the distress of those days "the sun will be darkened, and the moon will not give its light; the stars will fall from the sky, and the heavenly bodies of the heavens will be shaken". At that time the sign of the Son of Man will appear in the sky, and all the nations of the earth will mourn. They will see the Son of Man coming on the clouds of the sky, with power and great glory' (Matthew 24:29-30).[1]

Be careful of literalism ...

Especially where cosmic upheavals are described. Isaiah did not mean it literally when he said: 'The stars of heaven and their constellations will not show their light. The rising sun will be darkened

REMEMBER THIS

and the moon will not give its light' (Isaiah 13:10). It is a graphic way of indicating God's power at work behind the scenes of human history (the destruction of Babylon).

We encounter difficulties if we take Joel's 'cosmic convulsions' literally: 'I will pour out my Spirit in those days. I will show wonders in the heavens and on the earth, blood and fire and billows of smoke. The sun will be turned to darkness and the moon to blood before the coming of the great and dreadful day of the LORD' (Joel 2:29-31). This was fulfilled at Pentecost (see Acts 2:16-21). Again, these cosmic disturbances are a literary device, a graphic way of stressing the activity of God behind the scenes. Here, God kept the promise to pour out his Spirit. To rightly interpret such things, we need to understand both the immediate context and the harmony of the whole Bible.

As in all theophanies, almighty God condescends to our weakness, appearing in a manner that mortals can cope with, for 'No one may see [God] and live' (Exodus 33:20). God must *conceal* himself even as he *reveals* himself. God is so awesome, so pure, so holy, so immense and so unlike any other being, that if he appeared without some form of concealment, men would die. His appearing would not benefit but destroy man. God must wrap his transcendent majesty in a mantle of some sort. The concealment may be a mantle of fire and smoke or thunder and lightning (at Sinai and for Job). It may be a burning bush, or hiding Moses in the cleft of a rock so he saw only 'the backward parts' (a little glimpse) of God. Or it may be a mantle of human nature (as with the Angel of the Lord, and at the incarnation of Christ). God was clothed in a pillar of cloud or a pillar of fire at the Exodus. In each case the 'concealing in revealing' was an act of mercy. It is humbling to realize that even when God comes near to bless us, he must still keep some distance to protect us!

Keeping this wider context in view, 'the storm' really represents 'the Lord'. This storm, which ended all Job's troubles, is reminiscent of the storm that started his troubles, killing his family (1:19). Job knew God was in that storm too, for he immediately interpreted it as 'The LORD gave, and the LORD has taken away'. Either way, the storm leads us to Yahweh himself.

2. A proper view of God

Job came to a more mature view of God. He found that knowing God was a sufficient answer to all his questions. All the 'unknown' things become insignificant when you know the God who knows all things. That is what Elihu prepared Job to learn. That is what God's words in the storm declare, and that is what you and I must come to, not only once in a lifetime, but over and over again. A proper view of God produces two particular fruits:

1. A sense of proportion

Things that seem major and vexing to us humans must be seen in the shadow of the Almighty, so that they appear in their right proportion. The most massive 'fact' in the universe is God himself. Other facts seem insignificant compared to him. Job was struggling with a fact, a very real and distressing problem: why is a righteous man suffering so terribly? We should not minimize it. We are moved by his severe afflictions. Our sympathies are justifiably with him. He has major questions. He is understandably anxious to ask God for answers. His life is quite preoccupied and thoroughly distracted with these ongoing perplexities. But look at what happened when his opportunity finally came and he saw God. Everything changed! He acquired a whole new sense of proportion, a whole new outlook. Though still in pain and still ignorant of the reasons, he met God and he knew God. His very urgent questions were no longer burning issues. A real calm and contentment settled over him. It changed his frame of mind, contrasting with his turmoil and restlessness in the previous weeks and months. 'I despise myself and repent in dust and ashes' (42:6).

Let us learn that the answers to Job's most vital questions (and ours) do not come as a neat set of logical propositions from heaven. Rather, they are sufficiently answered in knowing God. God is a sufficient answer, a massive answer, to all our little and big concerns. Indeed, God's appearing only brought more questions onto the agenda. Did you notice? In the storm God interrogated Job with question after question (seventy-seven have been counted). God knows all the answers to all the questions, but Job had to come to the point of resting easy in God! The answer to all our 'hows' and 'whys' is not propositional but personal. It is the knowledge of God. That leads to a true sense of proportion. So we sing:

> O Lord my God! When I in awesome wonder
> Consider all the works Thy hands have made,
> I see the stars, I hear the mighty thunder
> Thy power throughout the universe displayed;
> Then sings my soul, my Saviour God, to Thee,
> How great Thou art!

So if you truly know God, it makes no difference that you have many unsolved mysteries, many questions unanswered. Your faith, like Job's, will still stand firm. The reason some people have a low view of Scripture (not believing its contents) is that they do not know God. Their 'god' is too small. Even in heaven we will have many unanswered questions. We will never know all things like God. We will have even more questions then than now, because only then will we realize the extent of God's universe and the little we know of it. Then the unsearchable riches of Christ will be more obvious, causing us to wonder even more. But all those questions are 'academic': we will keep on seeing God who is a sufficient answer. Let us get into that mode now, seeing and knowing him now. And then we can rest, putting away anxiety and frustration.

2. A sense of fear

Knowing God brings a sense of holy fear, a sense of wonder, an awareness of standing on holy ground. The presence of God is unmanageable. Scripture records some examples. Isaiah said, 'Woe to me! … and my eyes have seen the King' (Isaiah 6:5). The vulnerability of Manoah (Samson's father) was obvious: 'We are doomed to die! We have seen God!' (Judges 13:22). It was similar at Sinai: 'The sight was so terrifying that Moses said, "I am trembling with fear"' (Hebrews 12:21). John's filial bond with Jesus on earth took on a new dimension when he saw Jesus exalted in heaven: 'When I saw him, I fell at his feet as though dead' (Revelation 1:17). When he saw the miraculous draft of fish, Peter 'fell at Jesus' knees and said, "Go away from me, Lord; I am a sinful man!"' (Luke 5:8).

Similarly, Job was greatly humbled, despising himself. Being near to God is no trivial thing!

Having God near to us is an act of mind-boggling proportions. That explains the 'keep your distance' protocols in the Old Testament. It happened to Moses at the burning bush: '"Do not come any closer," God said. "Take off your sandals, for the place where you are standing is holy ground"' (Exodus 3:5). Joshua too was told: 'Take off your sandals, for the place where you are standing is holy' (Joshua 5:15). Who could forget Sinai? 'Mount Sinai was covered with smoke, because the LORD descended on it in fire ... the whole mountain trembled violently ... and the LORD said to him, "Go down and warn the people so they do not force their way through to see the LORD and many of them perish. Even the priests, who approach the LORD, must consecrate themselves, or the LORD will break out against them"' (Exodus 19:18-22).

We need to recapture a sense of this strict protocol, especially because of the greater privileges we now enjoy under the gospel. In Christ, God has not only drawn near to us: he has become one of us, a man, Immanuel. He has stopped saying, 'Keep your distance, do not approach, do not touch.' On the contrary, he now says, 'Come to me, draw near to me and I will draw near to you.' He says, 'Open the door and I will come in and eat with you!' He says, 'Seek me and you shall find me.' The holiest place is open to us. We are now exhorted to 'approach the throne of grace with confidence' (Hebrews 4:16). That was out of bounds in the Old Testament! Our privileges are enormous. 'Therefore, brothers, since we have confidence to enter the Most Holy Place by the blood of Jesus, by a new and living way opened for us through the curtain, that is, his body, and since we have a great priest over the house of God, let us draw near to God with a sincere heart in full assurance of faith' (Hebrews 10:19-22).

But our familiarity with that has to be kept in check to avoid flippancy. It is dangerous to lose sight of God's holiness. Privilege can lead to presumption. God has not changed since the days of Job and Moses. The fact still remains: 'The LORD is in his holy temple; let all the earth be silent before him' (Habakkuk 2:20). The command has never changed: 'Serve the LORD with fear and rejoice with trembling' (Psalm 2:11). All who know him will say 'Amen' to that.

DISCUSS IT

QUESTIONS FOR DISCUSSION

1. *Read 1 Timothy 6:15-16. Can this be harmonized with Matthew 5:8?*

2. *Malachi predicted that Elijah would come again (read Malachi 4:5-6). How do the following texts prove that it was not literally Elijah: Matthew 11:12-14; 17:10-13; Luke 1:13-17; John 1:19-28?*

CHAPTER TWELVE

ALL CREATURES GREAT AND SMALL

LOOK IT UP

BIBLE READING

Job 38 - 41

INTRODUCTION

All Creatures Great and Small is the name of a book by James Herriot[1] (and a television series based upon it). But long before Herriot, it was the substance of a much greater speech by a much greater author. God spoke about it out of a tempest (Job 38 - 41).

In these speeches God fired question after question about the amazing mysteries in his creation. He claimed 'all creatures great and small' as his property. He made them. He understands them. He controls them. Job saw again that creation, and the study of it (science), involves myriads of marvellous truths about God. We can listen as God tells Job about:

1. The great creatures
2. The small creatures

1. The great creatures

There is much that staggers the mind in these chapters. Every verse confronts us with a new insight into the awesome power of God. He interrogated Job: 'Where were you when I laid the earth's foundation? Tell me, if you understand. Who marked off its dimensions? Surely you know! Who stretched a measuring line across it? On what were its footings set, or who laid its cornerstone — while the morning stars sang together and all the angels shouted for joy?' (38:4-7). The question is mind-blowing. Who drew up the blueprints of the cosmos? Who designed it and worked it all out prior to building? And, since there was nothing before it, what did it all hang on? How do you hang a massive thing like earth in thin air? How does 'nothing' become a suitable foundation on which to support 'everything'?

And while Job is floundering about that 'great creature', God moves right on with his speech: 'Who shut up the sea behind doors when it burst forth from the womb, when I made the clouds its garment and wrapped it in thick darkness, when I fixed limits for it and set its doors and bars in place, when I said, "This far you may come and no farther; here is where your proud waves halt"?' (38:8-11). Who made the seas, those voluminous depths and expanses of water, always surging and breaking and crashing, restlessly trying to break out? Even these two creatures (land and sea) are worthy of much more intensive thought.

There are two other great creatures worthy of our attention, not only because God directed Job's thinking about them for a considerable time, but because they are not well understood by readers. These are the *behemoth* (40:15-24) and the *leviathan* (41:1-34). God describes these as the greatest of all the animals: the behemoth is the greatest land animal and the leviathan the greatest sea animal.

The behemoth (בְּהֵמוֹת)

'Behemoth' means 'gigantic beast' or 'great monster', and scholars have laboured to identify him. They generally interpret him as the hippopotamus, elephant, or rhino. But those are impossible answers. They just do not fit the description in the text. There is no known living creature in our world that fits this picture:

> 'Look at the behemoth, which I made along with you and which feeds on grass like an ox. What strength he has in his loins, what power in the muscles of his belly! His tail sways like a cedar; the sinews of his thighs are close-knit. His bones are tubes of bronze, his limbs like rods of iron' (40:15-18).

The tails of elephants, hippos and rhinos are puny little stringy things, not 'like a cedar'.

'When the river rages, he is not alarmed; he is secure, though the Jordan should surge against his mouth. Can anyone capture him by the eyes, or trap him and pierce his nose?' (40:23-24). Even if a mighty river like Jordan in full flood should surge against his mouth, the behemoth is relaxed and happy. Other animals fear and get swept away. But this monster is unmoved! Even a strong current does not trouble him. Now this does not really fit the facts for rhinos, elephants or hippos. True, they enjoy a swim (especially hippos) but they prefer still water, water holes or gentle currents. They are strong on land, but their vast bulk and stocky legs with flat feet means they are easily swept away in a current. So what is 'behemoth'?

The leviathan (לִוְיָתָן)

It is often assumed the leviathan is either the crocodile or whale. However, there is absolutely no way you can fit those animals into the descriptions given here. 'Can you pull in the leviathan with a fishhook or tie down his tongue with a rope? Can you put a cord through his nose or pierce his jaw with a hook?' (41:1-2). You cannot pull the leviathan with a hook or tie down his mouth with rope but that is exactly what is done with crocodiles! 'Can you fill his hide with harpoons or his head with fishing spears?' (v. 7). Yes, that is precisely what subdues whales and crocodiles! Obviously the leviathan is much greater than whales or crocodiles.

'The sword that reaches him has no effect, nor does the spear or the dart or the javelin. Iron he treats like straw and bronze like rotten wood. Arrows do not make him flee; slingstones are like chaff to him. A club seems to him but a piece of straw; he laughs at the rattling of the lance' (41:26-29). The truth is that crocodiles and whales have been hunted so successfully with ropes and harpoons that they are an endangered species in some places. But the leviathan, never! There is no way you can catch this monster. He laughs and defies every attempt by puny man.

'Any hope of subduing him is false; the mere sight of him is overpowering' (41:9). But zoos are full of crocodiles. Marine parks have plenty of killer whales in stock. Perfume companies have butchered millions of whales. We need to be sobered again by the description of this monster.

> 'I will not fail to speak of his limbs, his strength and his graceful form. Who can strip off his outer coat? Who would approach him with a bridle? Who dares open the doors of his mouth, ringed about with his fearsome teeth? His back has rows of shields tightly sealed together; each is so close to the next that no air can pass between. They are joined fast to one another; they cling together and cannot be parted. His snorting throws out flashes of light; his eyes are like the rays of dawn. Firebrands stream from his mouth; sparks of fire shoot out. Smoke pours from his nostrils as from a boiling pot over a fire of reeds. His breath sets coals ablaze, and flames dart from his mouth. Strength resides in his neck; dismay goes before him. The folds of his flesh are tightly joined; they are firm and immovable. His chest is hard as rock, hard as a lower millstone. When he rises up, the

mighty are terrified; they retreat before his thrashing. The sword that reaches him has no effect, nor does the spear or the dart or the javelin. Iron he treats like straw and bronze like rotten wood. Arrows do not make him flee; slingstones are like chaff to him. A club seems to him but a piece of straw; he laughs at the rattling of the lance. His undersides are jagged potsherds, leaving a trail in the mud like a threshing-sledge. He makes the depths churn like a boiling cauldron and stirs up the sea like a pot of ointment. Behind him he leaves a glistening wake; one would think the deep had white hair. Nothing on earth is his equal — a creature without fear. He looks down on all that are haughty; he is king over all that are proud' (41:12-34).

So what are the behemoth and the leviathan? The reason commentators cannot identify them is because they are extinct. Modern Bible scholarship has become so polluted with the dogmas of evolutionary geology that it never occurs to men that mankind once lived in the same world as monstrous animals that we know about only from their fossils!

It's a question of authority.

Our attitude to Scripture is on trial here. Is it reliable, being God's Word? Is it authoritative for my world view? The Bible clearly teaches that all animals, living or extinct, were made on days five and six of the creation week. So they were made alongside man, who was given dominion over them all (the behemoth and leviathan included). There was no danger to man until he fell in sin. Then all sorts of dangers arose, because the whole creation was affected and cursed. This has major implications for interpretation.

The most likely explanation is that the behemoth and leviathan were *dinosaurs*! What we know of the dinosaur fossils makes perfectly good sense in the Job text. The popular evolutionary myth that dinosaurs became extinct about seventy million years before man is utterly fallacious. God made the behemoth with man. They lived alongside each other! Job obviously knew what one looked like because God told Job to 'Look at Behemoth', (הִנֵּה־נָא בְהֵמוֹת). Consider him, think about him!

What sorts of dinosaurs were they? There are a few possibilities. *Tyrannosaurus* had a head five feet long, and it seems he could open his mouth four feet wide. He had a powerful body about fifty feet long and twenty feet tall. His assumed weight was ten tons! *Brontosaurus* was seventy feet long, weighing forty tons, but he was not as big as *Brachiosaurus,* which is the biggest anyone has found yet. He weighed ninety tons, was eighty feet long, standing twenty feet high at the shoulders and forty feet at the head (that is a four-storey building).

Why are they extinct? Scientists are mystified to explain why these strongest and biggest of all creatures have entirely perished from the face of the earth, while millions of tiny, smaller and much weaker creatures have survived and proliferated. It surely argues against 'survival of the fittest'.

We must look to the flood of Noah. Presumably these massive creatures were not in the Ark. If they did not drown or perish from lack of food in the deluge or from sheer fatigue as the swirling waters covered the mountains, they ended up in their fossil graveyard for some reason associated with the Flood. We cannot recount all the events of ancient history with dogmatic accuracy. Whatever the details of dinosaur history were, the data available to us suggests that Job had seen one.

What about this: 'His snorting throws out flashes of light; his eyes are like the rays of dawn. Firebrands stream from his mouth; sparks of fire shoot out. Smoke pours from his nostrils as from a boiling pot over a fire of reeds. His breath sets coals ablaze, and flames dart from his mouth' (41:18-21).

It cannot be confidently asserted that dinosaurs did not breathe fire. We do not know what dinosaurs could do. It is largely guesswork! Certain insects can create explosions, light and heat (like the Bombardier beetle). In fact dinosaur fossils have been discovered with a strange protuberance on the top of their head, and an internal cavity within. It is at least possible that it served as a mixing chamber for various combustible gases or chemicals, which, if suddenly exhaled by the beast, might ignite with the oxygen in the air. Only an arrogant man would say 'impossible', especially given the amazing capacity of the Bombardier beetle. It mixes up two chemicals, Hydrogen Peroxide and Hydroquinone — very explosive! But, it also has an inhibiter to stop the bang from harming itself. When an enemy attacks, the Bombardier beetle squirts out the mixture without the inhibitor, producing an explosion of hot, irritating, bad-smelling gases. Ancient history from all parts of the world has accounts of 'fire-breathing dragons'. We would be foolish to write off all these accounts as fictitious nonsense. It is unscientific to dismiss things because either we do not understand how they worked or they are not here now.

The Bible uses this sort of monster, this terrible dragon that man fears and cannot conquer, to depict Satan. He is the 'enormous red dragon with seven heads and ten horns and seven crowns on his heads. His tail swept a third of the stars out of the sky and flung them to the earth' (Revelation 12:3-4). What better symbol could be chosen? Man has no weapons against that monster. But God does. God can and does crush his head through his Son Jesus Christ.

2. The small creatures

Size is relative, but compared to the behemoth and leviathan, the other animals mentioned by God here are small, like the lion, ox, donkey, goat, eagle, horse and ostrich. I draw attention to two of them because they are compared and contrasted in the text and also because they show the marvellous variety in God's world.

The horse

What a marvellous animal the horse is! Even novices, who have no experience with them and feel quite uneasy on their backs, can appreciate their beauty and strength. We love to see a spirited steed throw back its head, stamp in defiant arrogance, and whinny and gallop with strength to burn! God draws particular attention to the military horse, which has been specially picked for its ability.

> 'Do you give the horse his strength or clothe his neck with a flowing mane? Do you make him leap like a locust, striking terror with his proud snorting? He paws fiercely, rejoicing in his strength, and charges into the fray. He laughs at fear, afraid of nothing; he does not shy away from the sword. The quiver rattles against his side, along with the flashing spear and lance. In frenzied excitement he eats up the ground; he cannot stand still when the trumpet sounds. At the blast of the trumpet

he snorts, "Aha!" He catches the scent of battle from afar, the shout of commanders and the battle cry' (39:19-25).

Yet, for all his beauty, the horse is a mere creature of God. It is good to have a true appreciation of the horse, but never neglect the creator. Yet men do. They marvel and devote themselves to horses, while denying and ignoring the God who made horses out of nothing! What folly!

The ostrich

What a contrast to the horse! That strange bird has been called 'one of God's jokes'. 'The wings of the ostrich flap joyfully, but they cannot compare with the pinions and feathers of the stork. She lays her eggs on the ground and lets them warm in the sand, unmindful that a foot may crush them, that some wild animal may trample them. She treats her young harshly, as if they were not hers; she cares not that her labour was in vain, for God did not endow her with wisdom or give her a share of good sense. Yet when she spreads her feathers to run, she laughs at horse and rider' (39:13-18).

This curious bird flaps its feathers but cannot fly. It is the largest living bird (weighing up to 300 pounds), the only bird with two toes and eyelashes, with huge eyes on a long neck. It looks like a periscope on legs. God admits that he did not give her wisdom or a share of good sense.

She is not a particularly good 'mother'. She lays her eggs on the ground without giving any thought to how easily they will be crushed and trampled! She does not appear to have much 'maternal instinct'. Having laid her eggs she abandons them! This is most unlike other birds, which take exquisite care of their young. The 'father' ostrich is more responsible. He sits on the nest. He guards it and distracts predators!

The Arabs have various insulting proverbs about ostriches regarding the fact that the female ostrich sometimes hides her head in foliage, as if she was in no danger from an enemy she cannot see! Hence, our warning: 'Do not bury your head in the sand.' All in all, she cannot fly, she is lacking in brains, and she is not a good mother; but God gave her a unique gift: running fast! She can run at 40 mph (64 kph) and not just for a short distance! 'God did not endow her with wisdom, or give her a share of good sense, yet when she spreads her feathers to run, she laughs at horse and rider.' John Williamson has captured the Australian equivalent well in his song about 'Old Man Emu': 'Emu can't fly, but I'm telling you he can run the pants off a kangaroo.'

Curious thing! That is the whole point! Like Job, we have to learn that God has questions we cannot answer. How and why did he make a creature like the ostrich? Why create something so outlandish and yet so brilliant and capable in its own particular strong point — running! Whether it is ants or elephants, orbits or ostriches, beetles or *brachiosaurs*, monsters or molecules, they all display the handiwork of God. All creatures great and small are God's creatures. They all reveal the Creator and because he alone has all the answers, we must feel our own smallness and insignificance. If we humbly marvel at God we will be as wise as Job. May it be so!

DISCUSS IT

QUESTIONS FOR DISCUSSION

1. *What are the consequences of denying creation? (See Psalm 24:1; John 1:1-14; and Hebrews 1:1-2.)*

2. *Since the doctrine of 'creation out of nothing' is a matter of faith, why is it inexcusable to deny it? (See Hebrews 11:3; Psalm 19:1-6; and Romans 1:18-20.)*

3. *Count the number of times the term 'God said' occurs in the first chapter of Genesis. With that in mind, how do you respond to the claim: 'The Bible does not tell us how God did it (creation) only that he did it'?*

CHAPTER THIRTEEN

'HE EXALTS THE HUMBLE'

LOOK IT UP

BIBLE READING

Job 42

INTRODUCTION

The Virgin Mary praised God's operating principle: 'He has lifted up the humble' (Luke 1:52). Jesus expressed it in universal terms: 'Everyone who exalts himself will be humbled, and he who humbles himself will be exalted' (Luke 14:11). The end of the book of Job is a case in point. Job was a humble, righteous man who endured traumatic physical pain in his flesh and terrible emotional pain from inept counsellors. As we readers look on, Job wins our admiration throughout the long ordeal. Yes, he said some improper things during his sojourn in agony, but that makes him one of us. He's human. We warm to him. We identify with him. Yet he exceeds us. We sense that Job did better than any of us would have done in the circumstances. He never once cursed God or impugned his integrity. At the end of forty-one chapters we wonder how much longer this agony must go on. Will it ever end? We have seen abundant evidence of humility in Job. Will God's *modus operandi* show up here at last? Will he exalt the humble? Yes, and the epilogue records it (chapter 42). God exalted the humble. This record of Job's recovery has three segments:

1. His summation
2. His vindication
3. His restoration

1. Job's summation (vv. 1-6)

'Then Job replied to the LORD: "I know that you can do all things; no plan of yours can be thwarted. You asked, 'Who is this that obscures my counsel without knowledge?' Surely I spoke of things I did not understand, things too wonderful for me to know. You said, 'Listen now, and I will speak; I will question you, and you shall answer me.' My ears had heard of you but now my eyes have seen you. Therefore I despise myself and repent in dust and ashes."'

Since these are Job's last recorded words, and since they sum up his most mature state of mind after hearing God's momentous speeches, it is important that we understand him. The real difficulty arises in his last sentence. Evidently Job shows contrition, for he uses the verb 'despise' (אֶמְאַס). Underlying all its various nuances, this word denotes the idea of abhorring, recoiling, rejecting, refusing or despising. But no object is provided for this verb in the Hebrew text. The question is: *What* does Job despise?

Some English translations supply the word 'myself' as the object: 'Therefore I despise *myself*. That is debatable. The context suggests that Job despised the rash and ignorant things he had said during his ordeal. He has just admitted it: 'Surely I spoke of things I did not understand, things too wonderful for me to know.' He admitted that he had obscured God's counsel. He owned up to some silly comments. The word 'therefore' is a significant clue because it links his feeling of horror to those things he wished he had never said, the things he now regrets. Literally, Job said, 'Therefore I despise'. This is not personal deprecation. This is not Job loathing himself but loathing his mistakes. He is recoiling from them. A more accurate translation would be: 'Therefore I retract' (NASB). The meaning (implied by the context) is: 'Therefore I retract those words … I withdraw them, I despise them, I fall from them.'

An important implication follows. Job is *not* saying, 'I now wish to concede that my suffering was deserved after all, though I used to deny it.' The sins he confesses here happened *after* the sufferings began, so they cannot possibly be the cause of his pain. He admits speaking wrongfully during his trial, so how can that be what the trial was originally intended to punish? His other expression, 'and I repent' (וְנִחַמְתִּי), is a parallel way of saying the same thing. In other words, Job is saying, 'I despise the things I said so foolishly. Though I was in pain, that is no excuse, so I repent of my remarks.'

REMEMBER THIS

Why is this important?

Otherwise we will ruin the whole story. We will end up proving the three counsellors right and Job wrong! We will conclude that Job has finally admitted to their persistent argument that his sins lie at the bottom of all his sufferings! But that is impossible because God is about to give the opposite verdict.[1]

So Job has shown great humility in admitting his foolish words. The encounter with God in the storm has matured and sanctified him further. He deeply regrets any offence to God. Though he is still in the dark as to why he suffered, he is right in maintaining his innocence. His experience is, from man's perspective, anomalous. It is one of the mysteries of providence. There is no reason for Job to change his plea. That does not contradict his humble confession of personal sin. As with all good theology, Job's summation is based on fine distinctions, enlightened by the whole revelation of God.

2. Job's vindication (vv. 7-9)

'After the LORD had said these things to Job, he said to Eliphaz the Temanite, "I am angry with you and your two friends, because you have not spoken of me what is right, as my servant Job has. So now take seven bulls and seven rams and go to my servant Job and sacrifice a burnt offering for yourselves. My servant Job will pray for you, and I will accept his prayer and not deal with you according to your folly. You have not spoken of me what is right, as my servant Job has." So Eliphaz the Temanite, Bildad the Shuhite and Zophar the Naamathite did what the LORD told them; and the LORD accepted Job's prayer.'

Clearly, Job has won the long debate! 'Job has spoken of me what is right.' Again, this does not deny Job spoke some unwise words, but the crux of his argument was right, namely, that God's purposes in all events are just and wise, but often inscrutable and mysterious to us.

Human reason cannot perceive the secret ways of God. The three counsellors ignored this truth, but Job constantly brought them back to it, providing them with numerous examples, and repeatedly challenging them to explain various anomalies in life. God endorsed Job's thesis. Even Job's worst statements are less reprehensible than the simplistic haughty arrogance of his three friends.

There are several matters of irony here. First, by insisting that God was treating Job as a great sinner, thus punishing him, it was *the three friends* (not Job) who unwittingly charged God with injustice and cruelty. They implicated God through their 'holier than thou' presumptions. It is one thing to express a wrong opinion; it is another thing to claim God agrees! They accused Job of impugning God's justice because he kept protesting his innocence. The ironic fact is God had said from the start that Job *is* innocent. Not surprisingly, God said, 'I am angry with you ... because you have not spoken of me what is right.'

A second irony lies in the fact that they assumed Job was out of God's favour, that God was angry with him. It turns out that Job was never out of God's favour. God was not angry with Job! It is the three of them who made God angry! 'I am angry with *you*' (v. 7). And now they can only be restored to divine favour through the intercession of the man they had been oppressing! The tables have turned completely. 'How the mighty have fallen!' (2 Samuel 1:19).

At no point during the debate did it occur to them that *they*, not Job, might be the objects of God's wrath! Not once did it cross their minds that *they* were the ones in need of grace and forgiveness. They were so determined to give Job the benefits of their ministry that it did not occur to them that they actually needed *his* services! But God set the record straight: 'My servant Job will pray for you, and I will accept his prayer and not deal with you according to your folly.'

The vindication of Job is rich with gospel themes. We see a sacrifice for sin, a mediator's intercession, and God's servant ('my servant').

Sacrifice for sin

God told the three men: 'Take seven bulls and seven rams and go to my servant Job and sacrifice a burnt offering for yourselves.' Sin is a deadly thing. The penalty for sin is death: 'the wages of sin is death' (Romans 6:23).

The remission of sin also requires death. 'Without the shedding of blood there is no forgiveness' (Hebrews 9:22). In mercy, God accepts the death of a substitute, the shedding of innocent blood on behalf of the guilty.

In the days before Christ the sacrifices were animals. They are innocent since they do not 'sin'. They are not creatures of the moral realm (they are not accountable to God for right or wrong). And for that same reason, animal sacrifices had no saving merits: 'It is impossible for the blood of bulls and goats to take away sins' (Hebrews 10:4). They typified the only innocent sacrificial blood there is, the blood of Christ. 'He entered the Most Holy Place once for all by his own blood, having obtained eternal redemption' (Hebrews 9:12).

God commanded the three men to act as their own priests by offering the sacrifices themselves. This is further evidence that the book is set in the patriarchal times, before Sinai, before Moses, and before Jewish ceremonial worship.

A mediator's intercession

God appointed Job as the mediator to intercede with prayers for the guilty trio. Truly, the mercy of God is beyond words! Though they have offended him, he not only appoints the mediator to advocate on their behalf, but he pledges his acceptance of that intercession even before it happens. 'I will accept his prayer and not deal with you according to your folly.' It is also marvellous to see that Job had no malice towards them. He bore no grudge. They had caused him great distress, but he treated them with dignity and grace, not as they deserved. This is a faithful picture of our great Mediator, Jesus Christ. His prayers prevail for us. His blood cleanses us from all sins. He does not treat us according to our deserts, but in mercy.

'My servant'

It is significant that God calls Job 'my servant' (עַבְדִּי) four times in succession. This is also an unmistakable redemptive theme. It connects with the 'servant songs' of Isaiah.[2] The essence of the 'servant' theme is that God's righteous anger at the sins of his people can only be placated by his chosen servant giving himself as an innocent sacrifice on their behalf. The gospel is all about God's key man, 'my servant', Jesus. Isaiah states it this way: 'After the suffering of his soul, he will see the light of life and be satisfied; by his knowledge my righteous servant will justify many, and he will bear their iniquities. Therefore I will give him a portion among the great, and he will divide the spoils with the strong, because he poured out his life unto death, and was numbered with the transgressors. For he bore the sin of many, and made intercession for the transgressors' (Isaiah 53:11-12). So again the book of Job points beyond itself to Christ. It is rich with the paradigms of biblical typology.

3. Job's restoration (vv. 10-17)

'After Job had prayed for his friends, the LORD made him prosperous again and gave him twice as much as he had before. All his brothers and sisters and everyone who had known him before came and ate with him in his house. They comforted and consoled him over all the trouble the LORD had brought upon him, and each one gave him a piece of silver and a gold ring. The LORD blessed the latter part of Job's life more than the first. He had fourteen thousand sheep, six thousand camels, a thousand yoke of oxen and a thousand donkeys. And he also had seven sons and three daughters. The first daughter he named Jemimah, the second Keziah and the third Keren-Happuch. Nowhere in all the land were there found women as beautiful as Job's daughters, and their father granted them an inheritance along with their brothers. After this, Job lived a hundred and forty years; he saw his children and their children to the fourth generation. And so he died, old and full of years.'

The text does not actually say that God healed Job from the terrible satanic afflictions, those 'painful sores from the soles of his feet to the top of his head' (2:7). But it is obviously implied in 'the Lord made him prosperous again'. The writer links Job's restoration to his ministry of intercession, not his repentance. 'After Job had prayed for his friends, the Lord made him prosperous again.' It does *not* say, 'After Job had repented the Lord made him prosperous again', as if he had been afflicted in order to make him repent of sin. He was exalted after performing the merciful task of a mediator. The same paradigm is true for Christ: 'After he had provided purification for sins, he sat down at the right hand of the Majesty in heaven' (Hebrews 1:3). After humiliation comes exaltation. 'He exalts the humble'.

Job was no longer at the disposal of Satan as he had been during his time of humiliation. Though men could not see the cause of his humiliation, they could certainly see the effects. Job's low estate had been public and visible, so it was fitting that his exaltation should be public too. It would fall short of the demands of justice if Job were exalted privately, no matter how glorious it was. It is good to soar on wings of eagles in a hidden encounter with God. The apostle Paul described such an uplifting of the soul. He spoke of a man 'caught up to the third heaven. Whether it was in the body or out of the body I do not know ... caught up to paradise. He heard inexpressible things, things that man is not permitted to tell' (2 Corinthians 12:2-4). But it is difficult to see how Job's situation could be adequately resolved 'behind the scenes'. If it is unthinkable for Christ's exaltation to be anything less than public and visible, the same applies to Job who typifies Christ.

Once God had exalted him, no one doubted Job's integrity. 'All his brothers and sisters and everyone who had known him before came and ate with him in his house. They comforted and consoled him over all the trouble the LORD had brought upon him, and each one gave him a piece of silver and a gold ring' (v. 11). Once they shunned him and did not want to know him. Now they all acknowledge him with their love and gifts. Now he prospered more than ever: 'The LORD blessed the latter part of Job's life more than the first.'

THINK ABOUT IT

This is a paradigm of Christ's exaltation.

It too was public and visible, beginning with his resurrection. He appeared to more than 500 witnesses (1 Corinthians 15:6). His return will be visible like his ascension into heaven: 'This same Jesus, who has been

> taken from you into heaven, will come back in the same way you have seen him go into heaven' (Acts 1:11). Men shunned Christ in his state of humiliation but none will shun him in his glory. No one in the whole universe will dispute Christ's integrity then. Men will acknowledge the exalted Son of God far more profoundly than they acknowledged the exalted Job: 'Therefore God exalted him to the highest place and gave him the name that is above every name, that at the name of Jesus every knee should bow, in heaven and on earth and under the earth, and every tongue confess that Jesus Christ is Lord, to the glory of God the Father' (Philippians 2:9-11).

Some final observations are in order, first in relation to Job's three daughters. We should not read too much into their names. Jemimah means 'dove', Keziah means 'cinnamon', and Keren Happuch means 'horn of eye-paint', or in our idiom, 'jar of beauty cream'. There is greater significance in two other details mentioned: their beauty and inheritance.

Their beauty probably underscores Job's complete recovery. Job had been a very sick man but you would never know it by looking at his daughters. He has no traces of disease now. He did not father sickly or blemished children. On the contrary: 'Nowhere in all the land were there found women as beautiful as Job's daughters.'

Also, 'Their father granted them an inheritance along with their brothers.' That was not usually the case in a patriarchal system, where the estate of a father was apportioned to his sons. Even in the later Old Testament law, daughters only had an inheritance when there were no male heirs (Numbers 27:8). Job was probably expressing his gratitude for family life again. The story began with Job's profound love for his children. 'Early in the morning he would sacrifice a burnt offering for each of them, thinking, "Perhaps my children have sinned and cursed God in their hearts." This was Job's regular custom' (Job 1:5). So it is appropriate that the story ends with Job's profound love being shown to his children. It may also indicate the extent of his riches. God had blessed him so greatly that there was plenty to share between sons and daughters.

Secondly, it would be a misuse of this event to deduce that the sorrows of every believer will end in a similar 'happy ever after' way. Some Christians die in the midst of savagery and injustice. The correct application from Scripture is that, come what may, we are safe with God. Faith in God will never disappoint us, no matter what the appearance of things may be in this life. The Apostle said it well: 'Neither death nor life, neither angels nor demons, neither the present nor the future, nor any powers, neither height nor depth, nor anything else in all creation, will be able to separate us from the love of God that is in Christ Jesus our Lord' (Romans 8:38-39).

Finally, we should recall an important truth: 'A man's life does not consist in the abundance of his possessions' (Luke 12:15). Thus Job's greatest blessing was not his 'health and wealth' being restored abundantly. It was in seeing God (42:5) and in knowing God better (42:2). That is still true for us. 'Blessed are the pure in heart, for they will see God' (Matthew 5:8). 'Now this is eternal life: that they may know you, the only true God, and Jesus Christ, whom you have sent' (John 17:3).

QUESTIONS FOR DISCUSSION

1. *Read Luke 1:46-55. How many examples of God 'exalting the humble' are evident in Mary's song?*

2. *What features of the gospel can be seen in the prophetic 'servant' songs of Isaiah 42:1-4; 49:1-6; and 50:4-9?*

3. *From Matthew 24:23-27, how do we know Christ's return is unmistakable and public? What are some implications for the present age?*

4. *Read Hebrews 9 carefully. Was there any value in the Jewish temple sacrifices? If not, why not? If so, how?*

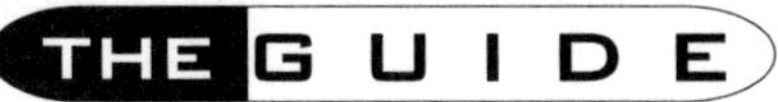

CHAPTER FOURTEEN

WHAT IS JOB ALL ABOUT?

LOOK IT UP

BIBLE READING

James 5:11

INTRODUCTION

How do we assess those forty-two chapters of intrigue, debate and innocent suffering? What do we make of that intense interplay of characters: God, Satan, Job, Eliphaz, Zophar, Bildad and Elihu? What is it all about? Can the essence of the story of Job be stated in a few words? Yes, we see it in James 5:11. It is the New Testament summary of the book of Job. In a short space James applies it to the daily lives of Christians, showing how it should affect their behaviour. What is Job all about? We will consider:

1. The New Testament answer
2. The New Testament application

1. The New Testament answer

'You have heard of Job's perseverance and have seen what the Lord finally brought about. The Lord is full of compassion and mercy' (James 5:11).

In essence the book of Job is all about the compassion and mercy of God! It is also about how God sovereignly rules and controls all events to bring about his 'intended end', his good plans and purposes. Let us take a closer look at both aspects of the answer.

1. Job is about God's mercy

The book of Job is all about God's mercy and compassion. It is all about the love, the kindness and the undeserved favour of God. The book of Job is all about 'good news' or 'gospel'. This might seem paradoxical and surprising, as it seems so full of 'bad news'. If asked: 'What is the book of Job all about?', many people would say, 'Job is about suffering', or 'Job is about the horrible things Satan can do to good people.' Invariably, the answer will focus on misery. But the New Testament does not give that answer. The inspired Word says Job is a book about compassion and mercy, not misery and suffering. Why?

It is vital that we feel the paradox. It involves the very heart of the gospel. The facts involved in the story of Job do not make sense by themselves. They certainly do not lead us to think of mercy and compassion. On the contrary, in themselves they are incongruous facts. They are shocking and outrageous facts; facts that alarm us. They demand an explanation. Unless there are good and significant reasons to explain the traumatic sufferings of Job, we feel a sense of injustice that such events ever took place. They do not sound good in court.

Job was a righteous man, the best on earth. He feared God and shunned evil. God drew Satan's attention to that fact. Then Satan accused Job before God. God allowed Satan to afflict Job terribly, and so Job became the innocent victim in a dispute between God and Satan. He became a real man of sorrows. None of his friends or kinsmen understood what was happening to him. Indeed, they aggravated his sufferings. They did not understand either Job's innocence or Satan's malice. Ordinary spectators would have to conclude that what happens to Job is tragic. Who would ever guess that it is all about God's love, compassion and mercy? How can God love Job if he allows (even initiates) such violence and injustice to be perpetrated against his servant? Why does he have to afflict Job in order to prove Satan wrong?

Where is the rationale, the interpretation, to explain these incongruous facts? It cannot be found in the book of Job. Even in the Old Testament as a whole the enigma remains. There are shadows, but shadows of what? It is only the coming of Christ that reveals the whole point of Job. Job is an Old Testament 'type' (pattern) of Jesus Christ. What happened to Job is what happened to Christ, in paradigm.

Job, the innocent man of sorrows, points to Christ, the innocent Man of sorrows. Job, in resisting the ancient serpent, points to Christ who crushed the serpent's head. God staked his reputation on Job. God's government rested on his shoulders. Will he stand firm? Yes, and he points to another man greater than Job: 'a child is born, to us a son given, and the government will be on his shoulders' (Isaiah 9:6).

The clearest evidence of the mercy and compassion of God is that he did not spare his Son Jesus Christ, but gave him up for our benefit. God gave his innocent Son to suffer terribly on the cross, the righteous for the unrighteous, and a substitute for the sins of others. Like Job, Christ did not suffer for sins of his own. Personal sin was not the explanation for personal suffering. He suffered what guilty men deserved, so they might be freed, pardoned and reconciled to God. That is the gospel. That is mercy, and that is what Job typifies, depicts and foreshadows. And that is why James interprets Job in terms of the mercy and compassion of God.

We all know that the real significance of people and events early in a story depends on later developments, and how it ends. Likewise, the first part of the Bible cannot be understood without the last part. The Old Testament does not make full sense without the New Testament. A strict Jew cannot understand the Old Testament because he refuses to accept the conclusion to its story (the New Testament). Christ is the key to all the Scriptures: 'The Scriptures ... testify about me' (John 5:39). The Old Testament events, histories and teachings lead ultimately to Christ. Jesus rebuked two men on the Emmaus Road for not understanding this. 'He said to them, "How foolish you are, and how slow of heart to believe all that the prophets have spoken!

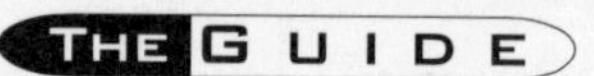

Did not the Christ have to suffer these things and then enter his glory?" And beginning with Moses and all the Prophets, he explained to them what was said in all the Scriptures concerning himself' (Luke 24:25-27).

REMEMBER THIS

What a privilege!

We have a big advantage over Job, namely, the privilege of hindsight. In a sense, we know Job better than he knew himself. He could not see his role in redemptive history. He could not read his book as part of the unfolding drama of sixty-six books. He had no idea that his experience was a remarkable paradigm of Christ's experience thousands of years later. That makes his endurance all the more admirable. It also makes our advantages all the more obvious. Praise God for placing our feet on such high ground. From that lookout we are privileged to see far more of the panorama of history. With greater privilege comes greater responsibility to honour God.

2. Job is about God's sovereignty

This second dimension of the book of Job is no less important. God is in control of all historical facts and events. He governs them all, and even when they seem paradoxical and confusing to us (as to Job) they belong to the wise plans of our sovereign God. That is what James says: 'You have seen what the Lord finally brought about.'

God has his secret purposes. Accordingly, he rules and overrules all things. Wickedness cannot frustrate those wise and holy purposes. 'God works for the good of those who love him, who have been called according to his purpose' (Romans 8:28). God causes the wickedness of Satan and his allies to fall upon their own heads and defeat them. God causes the evils done to and by his own chosen people to work ultimately for their good.

God is always in the driver's seat! God is always on the throne, always in control. Who would have thought so at the Red Sea, when Egypt closed in on Israel, leaving no way of escape? Who would have thought so when all Job's family and possessions were taken away? Who was thinking about God's sovereignty when his own Son was rejected by those he came to save? He was rejected, despised, misjudged and crucified by men. But, as always, everything was going to plan: 'This man was handed over to you by God's set purpose and foreknowledge; and you, with the help of wicked men, put him to death by nailing him to the cross. But God raised him from the dead, freeing him from the agony of death, because it was impossible for death to keep its hold on him' (Acts 2:23-24).

God used the death of Christ to accomplish the death of death. The outcome of 'no mercy' for Christ was 'full mercy' for all his people. When he struck the Head of the church Satan only succeeded in guaranteeing eternal life for the whole body. Spiritual malice only ensured liberty for all those under its enslaving power. In doing what he pleased (opposing Christ) Satan facilitated what he most hated (mercy, grace, pardon and forgiveness). So what is the book of Job all about? It is about God controlling all things to show his saving mercy and compassion. This has significant implications, as we shall see.

2. The New Testament application

It is one thing to know what the book of Job is all about, but it cannot stop there. It should bear fruit in our lives. Scripture is written not only to educate but also to train and equip us 'for every good work' (2 Timothy 3:16-17). Job can help to equip us in two practical areas of life.

1. Perseverance in trials!

Perseverance is hard when circumstances of life seem most unfair and oppressive. It is hard to persist in faith and godly obedience. But Job was oppressed and he stood firm. He is a model of perseverance. The reality is that God is still in control. He is still working his purposes out in your life! He is still bringing about his own ends, purposes and outcomes, which are all good, wise and perfect. He is still causing all things to work together for good for you, if you are one of his people. That includes the unjust things, the hurtful and unpleasant things, and the things that you cannot see any rhyme or reason for. No, the unpleasant things are not good, and the Bible is not suggesting that God makes them good. Rather, no event stands alone. All events 'work together'. God causes the pleasant and unpleasant things to intermesh for the good of his people and the destruction of his foes. We need to recognize this truth every day because it will not always feel like it! Just ask Job.

James applied the patient endurance of Job to his readers. The Christians he wrote to had suffered great injustice. They had worked hard as labourers, harvesting the fields of rich landowners, but after doing their work they were not paid. They were cheated by these rich swindlers. James warned the thieving landlords: 'Now listen, you rich people, weep and wail because of the misery that is coming upon you... Look! The wages you failed to pay the workers who mowed your fields are crying out against you. The cries of the harvesters have reached the ears of the Lord Almighty. You have lived on earth in luxury and self-indulgence... You have condemned and murdered innocent men, who were not opposing you' (James 5:1-6). But what advice did James give to their victims? How can they live peaceful godly lives in the face of such violent injustice against them?

Among other things, James tells them to follow Job's good example. 'Brothers, as an example of patience in the face of suffering, take the prophets who spoke in the name of the Lord. As you know, we consider blessed those who have persevered. You have heard of Job's perseverance and have seen what the Lord finally brought about' (James 5:10-11). The command 'be patient' (Μακροθυμήσατε) literally means 'be long suffering'. That is what God requires of us! Perhaps we are presently facing unpleasant circumstances, unfair and hurtful problems, trials producing fear and anxiety. So we worry and wonder and feel pressed down. Now what?

Be patient under trials! Hang in there! Do not despair! Do not try to judge the events without knowing their outcome! Do not think these things are 'just happening'. No! They are happening under God's control. He could stop them happening just as he could have stopped Job's anguish from happening. But while he chooses to do otherwise, you and I must treat God as God. Day by day and moment by moment we need to recall and actively submit to the truth that God is working his purposes out in our lives.

Unjust circumstances and hardships are no indication that he does not love us. He will bring glorious ends from it all but he has not told us how or when he will do it! And we are not to be merely 'resigned' to it. There is no honour in begrudgingly admitting, 'Okay, God's in control' while remaining 'uptight' or bitter and twisted. Rather, let it bring peace of mind and calmness of spirit. Let your mind dwell on these things and continue to serve God with all the zeal, commitment and joy he deserves from you. Of course, you should take whatever other steps are wise and responsible for redressing painful circumstances. The gospel does not preclude civil, legal and political remedies. But having done all, keep on submitting positively to the truth, rejoicing in the knowledge that God has everything in control.

2. Be clear on the role of Old Testament

Let the book of Job be a clear reminder that the gospel provides the correct grid for interpreting the Old Testament. We should always be asking one major interpretive question of any book in the Bible: How does it connect with Christ, or prepare for Christ, or foreshadow Christ? What lines does it draw which finally converge upon Christ? What principles of truth and mercy does it teach which have their fullest expression in Christ and the gospel? One thing is for sure: Christ is the key to all the Scriptures. Unless we use that key correctly, the Old Testament will appear to be of little relevance. The New Testament turns on the lights.

It has been well said, 'What was in the old concealed, now is in the new revealed.' What was latent in Old Testament is patent in New Testament. It is like a woman who is pregnant. At first the child in her womb is as tiny as the head of a pin. But even at this earliest stage its whole genetic make-up is there. All the adult will be is already contained in microscopic form in the little embryo. After a few months the mother can see her baby on a scan. A monitor shows the shadowy outline of the child. A close look reveals some details: the arms, the feet and the fingers can be identified. Later, when born, the reality is much clearer. Many details hidden in the womb are plain at birth. The Old Testament is the pre-birth scan of the New Testament child. Never forget that! This practical truth encourages better use of the Old Testament, as Christians read it more profitably and preachers expound it more correctly.

QUESTIONS FOR DISCUSSION

1. *'The greatest proof of God's mercy to the guilty is the greatest suffering inflicted on the innocent.' Is that correct? (See John 15:13; Romans 5:6-8; 8:32; 1 John 4:9-10.)*

2. *Study carefully 1 Corinthians 6:1-8. Some say it forbids Christians using civil courts for remedies against other professing Christians. Is that a correct understanding of the text in its context? Is the church competent to judge all matters of law (real estate, copyright, traffic, constitutions, contracts etc.)?*

3. *Hebrews 12:18-29 contrasts the inferior (Old Testament) form of God's kingdom with its superior (New Testament) form. What are the differences?*

THE GUIDE

NOTES

NOTES

NOTES

Chapter 1: Faith in the furnace

1. See her book *God's will is prosperity*, Harrison House, Tulsa Oklahoma, 1978.

Chapter 2: Job: the literary masterpiece

1. *Survey of the Old Testament and New Testament*, Russell Jones, p.163.

Chapter 3: Satan properly assessed

1. From the hymn 'A safe stronghold our God is still' by Martin Luther (1483-1546).

Chapter 6: Is God trustworthy?

1. From the hymn 'My hope is built on nothing less' by Edward Mote (1797-1874).

Chapter 7: The mystery of providence

1. For more explanation, see chapter 10, 'God in the storm'.
2. From the hymn 'And can it be?' by Charles Wesley (1707-1788).

Chapter 8: 'Where can wisdom be found?'

1. From the hymn 'Immortal, invisible, God only wise' by Walter C. Smith (1824-1908).

Chapter 10: Who is Elihu?

1. *The Communicator's Commentary*, Dr D. McKenna, Word Publishing, Vol. 12, 1986, pp. 225-6.

2. *Be Patient*, Dr Warren Wiersbe, Scripture Press, 1991, p. 123.
3. Dr Roy Zuck in *Everyman's Bible Commentary*, Moody Press, 1978, pp. 140-62.
4. S. B. Freehof, *Book of Job*, 1958, is so struck by the progress made in the Elihu narratives that he puts it down to a later writer who was so dissatisfied with the inconclusive nature of the arguments in the original book that he ventured to supply a better answer for Job than the three counsellors and even the Lord himself. To do this he invents Elihu as an entirely new character appearing out of nowhere, giving voice to orthodoxy, and representing the final revision of the book as we now have it. Freehof compares Elihu with a stage-struck young man who comes into an empty theatre and pretends to take part in a drama after all the actors have gone. (Freehof is so near to ... yet so far from, the truth.)

Chapter 11: God in the storm

1. Because the preceding verses (15-28) undoubtedly refer to the events of A.D. 70 it is sometimes assumed that Christ is still talking about the destruction of Jerusalem in verses 29-30. However, the words 'Immediately after the tribulation of those days' have to be understood in the light of Luke's more complete record of this Olivet Discourse. In particular: 'Jerusalem will be trampled underfoot by the Gentiles until the times of the Gentiles is fulfilled' (Luke 21:23-24). The judgement of God against Jerusalem is not over and done with in A.D. 70. It merely began then, starting an era known as 'the times of the Gentiles' (church history as we know it). It still continues. The times of the Jews are over, which means the national form of covenant administration (Judaism) has given way

to the international form (church of all nations). So 'the tribulation of those days' should not be restricted to A.D. 70. It announces a period of history extending right up to the very threshold of Christ's return. That is when 'the times of the Gentiles is fulfilled'.

How do we understand: 'when you see all these things, you know that he is near, right at the door' (Matthew 24:33)? Clearly Jesus is referring to the public and obtrusive nature of his glorious return. His immediately preceding words described it: 'They will see the Son of Man coming on the clouds of the sky, with power and great glory. And he will send his angels with a loud trumpet call, and they will gather his elect from the four winds, from one end of the heavens to the other'. They are not 'signs' preceding his advent to give people a final warning. Jesus plainly denies such precursory signs (vv. 36-39). Rather, they are events that *accompany* his advent. They are his entourage. They announce 'the King is here' (not 'he is coming').

Luke again provides the harmony: 'At that time they will see the Son of Man coming in a cloud with power and great glory. When these things begin to take place, stand up and lift up your heads, because your redemption is drawing near' (Luke 21:27-28).

Chapter 12: All creatures great and small

1. Herriot got his title from the hymn, 'All things bright and beautiful' by Cecil Frances Alexander (1823-95).

Chapter 13: 'He exalts the humble'

1. This point is well presented by Dr Frank Andersen, though he overstates it by claiming: 'Job confesses no sins here.' He confesses the sin of rash speech during his pains, but he does not confess any sins as the cause of those pains. See 'Job', *Tyndale Old Testament Commentary*, IVP, 1976, p.292.
2. See Isaiah 42:1-4; 49:1-6; 50:4-9; and 52:13 - 53:12.

A wide range of excellent books on spiritual subjects is available from Evangelical Press. Please write to us for your free catalogue or contact us by e-mail.

Evangelical Press
Faverdale North Industrial Estate, Darlington, DL3 0PH, England

Evangelical Press USA
P. O. Box 825, Webster, New York 14580, USA

e-mail: sales@evangelicalpress.org

web: www.evangelicalpress.org